WORLD FOLKTALES

An Anthology of Multicultural Folk Literature

Anita Stern

Victoria High School ESL

12

National Textbook Company
a division of NTC/CONTEMPORARY PUBLISHING GROUP
NTC Lincolnwood, Illinois USA

To my mother, Ida Enkel, for her endless help,
Yossi for his endurance,
Mickey and Tsafi for their technical support,
and Wanna Zinsmaster for her guidance.

Acknowledgments

"The Little Daughter of the Snow" by Arthur Ransome from *Old Peter's Russian Tales* (Jonathan Cape). Reprinted by permission of the Estate of Arthur Ransome.

"The Boy of the Red Sky" adapted from "The Boy of the Red Twilight Sky" by Cyrus Macmillan from *Canadian Fairy Tales* (The Bodley Head). Reprinted by permission of the Estate of Cyrus Macmillan.

"The Spoiled Child" adapted from "The Spoiled Daughter" by Radost Pridham from *A Gift from the Heart: Folk Tales from Bulgaria* (William Heinemann Ltd.).

"The Woodsman's Daughter and the Lion" adapted from "The Woodsman's Daughter" from *The Three Wishes: A Collection of Puerto Rican Folktales* by Ricardo E. Alegria, trans. Elizabeth Culbert (Harcourt, Brace & Co., Inc., 1969).

"The Lucky Charm" adapted from "The Sacred Amulet" from *Latin American Tales: From the Pampas to the Pyramids of Mexico* by Genevieve Barlow (Rand-McNally, 1966). Used by permission of Eiko Tien, Conservator for the Estate of Genevieve Barlow.

"Nazar the Brave" from *Once There Was and Was Not* by Virginia A. Tashjian, based on stories by H. Toumanian (Little, Brown, 1966). Used by permission of Virginia A. Tashjian.

"The Shah Weaves a Rug." From *The Elephant's Bathtub* by Frances Carpenter. Copyright © 1962 by Frances Carpenter Huntington. Used by permission of Doubleday, a division of Bantam Doubleday Dell Publishing Group, Inc.

"The Tiger's Whisker" from *The Tiger's Whisker and Other Tales and Legends from Asia and the Pacific* by Harold Courlander (Harcourt Brace & World, 1959. Copyright © 1959, 1987 by Harold Courlander). Used by permission of Harold Courlander.

"The Giant's Bride." Adapted from "The Giant's Bride" by Amabel Williams-Ellis from *Old World and New World Fairy Tales*, copyright © 1966 by Amabel Williams-Ellis. Published by Blackie Children's Books.

"The Love Crystal." Adapted from "The Love Crystal" from *The Fisherman and the Goblet* by Mark Taylor (Golden Gate Junior Books, 1971. Copyright © 1971 by Mark Taylor).

"The Blue Rose" by Maurice Baring. Printed by permission of A. P. Watt Ltd. on behalf of The Trustees of the Maurice Baring Will Trust.

"A True Hero" adapted from "The Noblest Deed" from *Tales the People Tell in Mexico*, copyright © 1972 by Grant Lyons. Reprinted by permission of Julian Messner, a division of Simon & Schuster, Inc.

"A Chief Names His Heirs" from *The Crest and the Hide and Other African Stories of Heroes, Chiefs, Bards, Hunters, Sorcerers and Common People* by Harold Courlander (Coward, McCann & Geoghegan, 1982. Copyright © 1982 by Harold Courlander). Reprinted by permission of Harold Courlander.

"The Skeleton's Dance" from *Folktales of Japan* by Seki (University of Chicago Press).

"The Voyage Below the Water" from *The Piece of Fire and Other Haitian Tales* by Harold Courlander (Harcourt Brace & World, 1964. Copyright © 1964, 1992 by Harold Courlander). Reprinted by permission of Harold Courlander.

Illustrations: Liz Sawyer, Simon Girling & Associates
Cover: Diane Novario

ISBN: 0-8442-0781-0

Published by National Textbook Company,
a division of NTC/Contemporary Publishing Group, Inc.,
4255 West Touhy Avenue,
Lincolnwood (Chicago), Illinois 60646-1975 U.S.A.
© 1994 by NTC/Contemporary Publishing Group, Inc.

8 9 0 VP 9 8

Understanding Key Words

Read the sentences. You will find words in **bold** in the story. Discuss what each word means.

1. The chief had fought in many battles and killed many enemies. He was a brave **warrior.**

2. The chief believed that he was the bravest of all, and he told his people this. He **bragged** that he was the best fighter.

3. The chief was pleased that he was the bravest of all. He was **proud** of himself.

4. The chief had a lot of power. The chief would give orders. The people in the village **obeyed** him.

5. When the baby was unhappy, it would cry and **scream.**

Words about the Time and Place

You will find these words in the story.

chief	the leader of a group or tribe
headdress	a covering for the head, made of feathers
maple sugar	the sweet liquid from a tree called the maple. It can be made into a kind of candy.
medicine bag	a bag in which magical things are kept. Native Americans believed that the magical things helped them have power over nature.
wigwam	a round house made of wooden poles that are covered with the bark of trees or animal skins. Some tribes built wigwams to live in.

Why the Baby Says "Goo"

In a village near the mountains, there lived a chief. He was a brave man who had fought in many battles. No one in the tribe had killed more enemies than he.

The chief feared no one. He fought the ice giants who came out of the North and carried away the women and children. He made them go back to their home in the North. He killed some of the evil people that lived in the caves, and he drove the others out of the land. Everybody loved the chief. He was so brave and good that the villagers thought there was no one like him anywhere.

But after he drove the giants out of the land, the chief began to think that he was the greatest warrior in the world.

"I can conquer anyone," he bragged.

Now a wise old woman lived in the village. When she heard what the great chief bragged, she smiled.

"Our chief is wonderful," she said, "but there is one who is more powerful than he."

The villagers told the chief what the wise woman had said. He came to visit her wigwam.

"Grandmother, who is this wonderful one?" he asked.

"His name is Wasis," answered the wise woman.

"And where is he, Grandmother?" asked the chief.

"He is there," said the wise woman, and she pointed to a place in the wigwam.

The chief looked. What do you think Wasis was? He was a fat little baby. He sat in the middle of the floor, talking to himself and sucking a piece of maple sugar. He looked so sweet and seemed very happy with himself.

The chief had no wife and knew nothing about babies. But he was very proud of himself, and he thought he knew everything. He was sure that the baby would obey him.

He smiled to little Wasis and said, "Baby, come to me!"

But the baby smiled and continued sucking his maple sugar.

The chief was surprised. The villagers always did everything he asked. He could not understand why the baby did not obey him. So he smiled and again said to little Wasis, "Baby, come to me!"

The baby smiled back and continued sucking his maple sugar.

The chief was surprised. No one had ever disobeyed him before. He grew angry. He gave little Wasis a mean look and shouted at him, "Baby, come to me!"

Little Wasis opened his mouth and began crying and screaming. The chief had never heard such awful sounds. Even the ice giants did not scream so terribly.

The chief was more and more surprised. He could not think why such a little baby would not obey him.

"Amazing!" he said. "All other men fear me. But this baby shouts back war cries. Perhaps I can control him with my magic."

He took out his medicine bag. He danced magic dances and sang wonderful songs.

Little Wasis smiled and watched the chief with big round eyes. He thought it was all very funny. But he continued to suck his maple sugar.

The chief danced until he was tired out. Sweat ran down his face. Red paint ran down his face and neck. The feathers on his headdress fell down.

At last, he sat down. He was too tired to dance any longer.

"Didn't I tell you that Wasis is stronger than you?" said the wise old woman. "No one is stronger than the baby. He always controls the wigwam. Everyone loves him and obeys him."

"So it is," said the chief sadly as he went out of the wigwam. As he went out, he could hear little Wasis talking to himself.

"Goo, goo, goo!" the baby said as he sucked his maple sugar.

Now when you hear a baby saying "Goo, goo, goo," you will know what it means. It is the baby's war cry. The baby is happy because he remembers the time when he won the battle with the chief in the wigwam of the wise old woman.

Understanding the Story

A. What Happens?

Match the sentence parts. Write the correct letter in each blank.

____ 1. Wasis is sucking	a. feathers in his headdress.
____ 2. The chief wears	b. the baby screams.
____ 3. The wise old woman asks	c. as terribly as the baby.
____ 4. Nobody in the tribe disobeys	d. a piece of maple sugar.
____ 5. The chief is	e. the chief.
____ 6. As the chief dances and sings,	f. the chief to visit her.
____ 7. The ice giants do not scream	g. he becomes tired.
____ 8. When the chief shouts,	h. sure the baby will obey him.

B. Looking Back

Answer these questions about the story.

1. Why is the chief respected by his tribe?
2. Why doesn't the baby obey the chief?
3. Why does the baby cry after the chief comes into the wigwam?
4. What surprises the chief about the baby?
5. Who is right—the wise old woman or the chief?

C. Understanding Characters' Feelings

Complete the chart. Tell how the chief and the baby feel at different times in the story. Use these words and other words that you know:

angry   disappointed   frightened   happy   sad   surprised   tired

	The Chief	**The Baby**
When the chief enters the wigwam:	*proud, confident*	
When the chief shouts:		
When the chief dances and sings:		
At the end of the story:		

Exploring the Meaning

A. Getting the Deeper Meaning

Discuss these questions about the story.

1. What does the chief learn?
2. What shows that the old woman is very wise?
3. At the end of the story the reader learns that the baby's war cry is "goo, goo, goo." What does this mean?
4. If the chief had been a father, he would have acted differently. What could have happened if he had children of his own?

B. Telling the Story Again

1. Imagine you are the chief. Tell the story from his point of view. Begin like this: "The people in my tribe told me that the wise old woman had said. . . ."

In your story, you can tell:

- why you thought the baby would obey you
- what you told the baby to do and what happened
- why you started to dance and what happened
- what you thought when you left the wigwam

2. Imagine you are the baby. Tell the story from his view. Begin like this: "One day I was sitting in the wigwam. . . ."

In your story, you can tell:

- who came into the wigwam
- what happened when you heard the chief shout
- what happened when the chief danced
- how you felt after the chief left the wigwam

C. In Everyday Life

Discuss these questions.

1. In what ways do parents control their children? In what ways can children control their parents?

2. In your native culture, how are babies treated? Who takes care of them?

3. In the story, the old woman is called wise by the tribe. How are older people treated in your native culture?

The Little Daughter of the Snow

Russian

Russia is famous for its long, hard winters. In some places, snow covers the ground and lakes and rivers are frozen for six months a year. You will see how snow and ice play an important part in this Russian folktale.

This tale tells about a magical child. Many cultures throughout the world tell stories about unusual children.

Before You Read

Discuss these questions.

1. What do you know about life in Russia?
2. What kinds of activities do people do outdoors in winter? Which of them have you done? Which would you like to do?
3. Why, do you think, is the story called "The Little Daughter of the Snow"? What will it be about?

Understanding Key Words

Read the sentences. You will find the words in **bold** in the story. Discuss what each word means.

1. The couple liked to **peep** out their window to see the children playing. They did not want the children to know that they were looking at them.

2. In the spring, the weather gets warmer. The snow **melts** and disappears.

3. The girl was lost and afraid. She shouted out. She asked anyone who heard to have **pity** on her. She wanted someone to feel sorry for her and help her.

4. The couple were **grateful** to the animal who helped their little daughter. They thanked the animal.

5. The couple thought, "If we give away the hen, we will get nothing back in return. This would be a **waste** of our nice hen."

Words about the Time and Place

You will find these words in the story.

birch	a kind of tree that has a thin trunk and a pale bark
fox	a wild animal that has a long, bushy tail
snowflake	a tiny piece of snow. Snow falls in flakes that have different shapes.
wolf	a wild animal that looks very much like a dog

The Little Daughter of the Snow

There were once an old man and his wife who lived in a little house in a village on the edge of the forest. They were unhappy because they had no children. They used to stand for hours, just peeping through their window to watch the childen of the village playing in the snow, laughing and shouting, making snow women.

The man said to the woman, "Wife, let us go into the yard and make a snow girl. Perhaps she will come alive, and be a little daughter to us."

"Husband," said the old woman, "there's no knowing what may be. Let us go into the yard and make a little snow girl."

So the couple put on their big coats and hats and began to make a little snow girl. They rolled up the snow to make her little arms and legs. They wanted their snow girl to be more beautiful than a birch tree in spring.

Toward the evening, she was finished—a little girl, all snow, with blind white eyes, and a tiny mouth, with snow lips tightly closed.

"Oh, speak to us," said the man.

"Won't you run about like the other children, little white pigeon?" said the woman.

Suddenly, in the twilight, they saw the snow girl's eyes shining blue like the sky on a clear day. Her lips flushed and opened, and she smiled. And there were her little white teeth. She had black hair that stirred in the wind.

She began dancing wildly in the snow, like snowflakes whirling in the wind. She tossed her long hair, and she started to laugh softly to herself. Her eyes shone, and she sang as the couple watched. This was her song:

"In my veins, no warm blood glows,
Only icy water flows;
Yet I'll laugh and sing and play

By frosty night and frosty day—
Little daughter of the Snow.

But this I do know
When you love me very little then
I shall melt away again.
Back into the sky I'll go—
Little daughter of the Snow.''

"Isn't she beautiful!'' said the man. "Run, Wife, and get a blanket to wrap her in.'' The woman got a blanket and put it around the shoulders of the little snow girl.

The man picked the snow girl up, and she put her little cold arms round his neck. "You must not keep me too warm,'' she said.

Well, the couple took her into their small house. She lay on a bench in the corner farthest from the stove, while the woman made her a little coat. The old man went to a neighbor and bought a fur hat and a pair of red boots for her. They dressed the little snow girl.

"Too hot, too hot,'' said the little snow girl. "I must go out into the cool night.''

"But you must go to sleep now,'' said the old woman.

"By frosty night and frosty day,'' sang the snow girl. "No, I will play by myself in the yard all night, and in the morning I'll play in the road with the children.''

Nothing the old people said could change her mind.

"I am the little daughter of the Snow,'' she replied as she ran out into the snow. She danced about in the moonlight on the white snow!

The couple watched her, but at last they went to bed. The man got up often during the night to make sure she was still there. And she was, running about in the yard, chasing her shadow in the moonlight and throwing snowballs at the stars.

In the morning, she came in, laughing, to have breakfast with the couple. She ate only a piece of ice, crushed into a small wooden bowl.

After breakfast, she ran out into the road to join the other children. The old couple watched her and were proud to see a little girl of their own out there playing.

How she played with the other children! She could run faster than

any of them. Her little red boots flashed as she ran about. And when the children made a snow woman, the little daughter of the Snow laughed like the ringing peals of little glass bells. The man and the woman watched her and were very proud.

"She is all our own," said the woman.

"Our little white pigeon," said the man.

In the evening, she ate another bowl of ice and went off again to play by herself in the yard.

"You'll sleep in our house tonight, won't you, my love?" asked the woman.

But the little daughter of the Snow only laughed with shining eyes. "By frosty night and frosty day," she sang and ran out the door.

And so it went on through the winter. The little daughter of the Snow sang and laughed and danced. She always ran out into the night and played by herself until the light of day. Then she'd come in and have her ice. And all day she'd play with the children.

She did everything the woman told her. Only she would never sleep indoors. All the children of the village loved her. They did not know how they had ever played without her.

It went on until the snow began to melt. Often the children went together a little way into the forest during the sunny part of the day. The little snow girl went with them. It would have been no fun without her.

One day they went too far into the woods. When the other children said they were going to turn back, the little snow girl tossed her head and ran on among the trees. The other children were afraid to follow her. It was getting dark. They ran home, holding each other's hands.

The little daughter of the Snow was out in the forest alone. She looked back for the others, but she could not see them. She climbed up into a tree, but she could not see them. Afraid, she called out, "Little friends, have pity on the snow girl."

A big brown bear heard her, and came tramping up to the tree on his heavy paws. "What are you crying about, little daughter of the Snow?"

"O Big Bear," said the little snow girl, "I have lost my way, and darkness is coming. All my friends are gone."

"I will take you home," said the big brown bear.

"O Big Bear," said the little snow girl, "I am afraid of you. I think you will eat me. I would rather go home with someone else."

So the bear left her.

A gray wolf heard her, and came galloping up on his quick legs. He asked her, "What are you crying about, little daughter of the Snow?"

"O Gray Wolf," said the little snow girl, "I have lost my way, and it is getting dark, and all my friends are gone."

"I will take you home," said the gray wolf.

"O Gray Wolf," said the little snow girl, "I am afraid of you. I think you will eat me. I would rather go home with someone else."

So the wolf left her.

A red fox heard her, and he came running up to the tree on his sturdy paws. He called out, "What are you crying about, little daughter of the Snow?"

"O Red Fox," said the little snow girl, "how can I help crying? I have lost my way, and it is quite dark, and all my friends are gone."

"I will take you home," said the red fox.

"O Red Fox," said the snow girl, "I am not afraid of you. I do not think you will eat me. I will go home with you, if you will take me."

So she came down from the tree, and she held onto the fox's back as they ran through the dark forest. Soon they saw the lights of the village and of the small house of the couple, who were inside crying.

"Oh, what has become of our little snow girl?"

"Oh, where is our little white pigeon?"

"Here I am," said the snow girl. "The kind red fox has brought me home. You must shut up the dogs so that they don't harm the fox." So the man shut up the dogs.

"We are very grateful to you," he said to the fox.

"Are you really?" said the red fox. "I am very hungry."

"Here is a nice piece of bread for you," said the old woman.

"Oh," said the fox, "I would like a plump hen. After all, your little snow girl is worth a plump hen."

"Very well," said the old woman, but she said to her husband: "We have our little girl again. It seems a waste to give away a plump hen."

"It does," said the old man.

The old woman told him what she meant to do. He went to get two sacks. In one sack, they put a plump hen, and in the other, they put their fiercest dog. They took the bags outside and called the fox. He came up to them, licking his lips, because he was hungry.

They opened one sack, and the hen fluttered out. The red fox was just about to grab her, when they opened the other sack, and out jumped the fierce dog. The poor fox saw the dog's eyes flashing in the dark, and he was so frightened that he ran back into the forest without eating the hen.

"That was well done," said the couple. "We have our little snow girl, and did not give away our plump hen."

Then they heard the little snow girl singing in the small house:

"Old ones, old ones, now I know
You love me less than a hen,
I shall go away again.
Good-bye, ancient ones, good-bye.
Back I go across the sky.
To my mother and father,
Little daughter of the Snow."

The couple ran into the house. There were a pool of water in front of the stove, a fur hat, a little coat, and tiny red boots. It seemed to the man and woman that they saw the snow girl with her bright eyes and long hair, dancing in the room.

"Do not go! Do not go!" they begged, but they couldn't see the little dancing girl. They could only hear her laughing and singing:

"Old ones, old ones, now I know
Less you love me than a hen,
I shall melt away again.
Away I go,
Little daughter of the Snow."

And just then the door blew open. A cold wind filled the room, and the little daughter of the Snow was gone. She jumped into the arms of Frost her father and Snow her mother, and they carried her away over the stars to the far north. There she plays all through the summer on the frozen seas. In winter, she comes back to Russia, and some day, when you are making a snow woman, you may find the little daughter of the Snow standing there instead.

Understanding the Story

A. Why Does it Happen?

Complete each sentence by choosing **a, b,** or **c.**

1. The man and his wife make the snow girl because
   a. it will be beautiful to look at.
   b. they hope it will come alive and be their daughter.
   c. the children will enjoy playing with it.

2. The little daughter of the Snow wants to be outside because she
   a. doesn't like the couple.
   b. wants to disobey.
   c. will melt if she gets too warm.

3. The little snow girl doesn't let the bear or wolf help her because she
   a. doesn't need help.
   b. wants the fox to help her.
   c. is afraid those animals will eat her.

4. The old woman doesn't give the fox a plump chicken because
   a. she is selfish.
   b. she has nothing to give.
   c. the fox does nothing to earn the chicken.

5. The couple lose their little daughter because
   a. the fox eats her.
   b. they treated the fox badly.
   c. the daughter gets lost and never returns.

B. Looking Back

Answer these questions about the story.

1. How do the couple get the snow girl?
2. What warnings does the snow girl give the couple when she arrives?
3. How is the snow girl different from the other children?
4. How is she like the other children?
5. How do the couple trick the fox?

C. *Understanding the Parts of the Story*

Complete the chart to show the main parts of the story.

The characters in the story (People/animals):	
Where the story takes place:	
Problems: 1. The couple's problem at the beginning of the story: How the problem is solved: 2. The problem the little daughter has in the forest: How the problem is solved: 3. The problem the couple has when the fox arrives: How the problem is solved:	1. 2. 3.
How the story ends:	

Exploring the Meaning

A. Getting the Deeper Meaning

Discuss these questions about the story.

1. How does the snow girl change the lives of the couple?
2. Why do the couple lose the snow girl?
3. What lesson do you think the story teaches?
4. Repeating parts of a story makes it easier to tell aloud. Look back at the section of the story in which the snow girl is lost in the forest. What parts are repeated?

B. Adding New Endings

1. Give the story a different ending. Tell what would happen if the couple gave the plump hen to the fox.
2. Tell what would happen if the fox tried to eat the snow girl.

C. In Everyday Life

Discuss these questions.

1. What challenges might parents have when they adopt older children rather than babies?
2. What kinds of misunderstandings can occur between parents and children?
3. What problems might a child have when he or she moves to a new neighborhood?

The Boy of the Red Sky

Canadian Indian

Many folktales try to explain something about nature: why the seasons come and go, why an animal looks or acts in a certain way, why the weather changes. This Canadian folktale explains why the sky is sometimes red.

This tale comes from the Indians, or Native Americans, who live in the northern part of North America. As you read, you will discover that, like "The Little Daughter of the Snow," this story tells about a special child.

Before You Read

Discuss these questions.

1. Many people believe that a red sky in the evening means that there will be nice weather the next day. Do you know any other signs that tell about the weather?

2. Have you ever been on a boat in the ocean? Have you ever been on a boat during a storm? Tell what happened.

Understanding Key Words

Read the sentences. You will find the words in **bold** in the story. Discuss what each word means.

1. The couple was lonely. They wanted a child to **keep** them **company.**

2. After the storm, the sea was very **calm and still.** There were no waves.

3. The magical boy could protect the man. When the man was with the boy, nothing could **harm** the man.

4. The man and woman were the boy's **foster parents.** They were not the boy's natural parents, but they took care of him as he grew up.

5. The woman would go to the beach at **twilight,** just as the sun was going down.

Words about the Time and Place

You will find these words in the story.

arrow	a stick with a sharp tip. It is used with a bow.
bow	a curved strip of wood or metal with a string. It is used to shoot arrows.
copper	a reddish-brown metal
kingfisher	a bird that lives near water and catches fish as its food
mist	small drops of water in the air. Mist can make it hard to see ahead.
salmon	a large fish with silver scales
sea gull	a large gray and white bird that lives near water
seashell	the hard outside covering of certain sea animals. Seashells are often found on beaches. Some Native Americans used them to decorate their clothing.

The Boy of the Red Sky

Long ago a young man and his wife lived near the Great Water in the west. They had no children, and they lived by themselves on an island, far from other people. The man caught deep-sea fish in the ocean and salmon in the rivers. He was gone for many days at a time, fishing. The woman was not afraid, but she was very lonely, looking each day at the gray sky and listening to the sound of the waves on the beach. Day after day she said to herself, "I wish we had children. They would be good company for me when my husband is far away."

One evening she sat alone on the beach at twilight, looking across the water. The sky was gray. Because she was so lonely, the woman said to herself, "I wish we had children to keep me company." At that moment, a kingfisher, with her family, was diving for food nearby. The woman said, "O Sea Bird, I wish I had children like you." The kingfisher replied by telling her to look at the seashells. The next evening a white sea gull was flying above the waves. The woman told the gull that she wished she had children. The sea gull replied, "Look at the seashells," and flew away.

The woman kept wondering about the words of the kingfisher and the sea gull. Suddenly she heard a strange cry coming from the sand behind her. When she came closer to the sound, she realized that the cry was coming from a large seashell lying on the sand. She picked up the shell and inside found a tiny boy, crying as hard as he could. The woman carried the baby home and took care of him. When her husband came home from the sea, he was very happy that she had found the baby. He knew that they would no longer be lonely.

The baby grew quickly. One day the child suddenly said to the woman, who was wearing a copper bracelet, "Please make a bow from the copper on your arm." She wanted him to be happy, so she made a tiny bow and two tiny arrows from the bracelet.

Every day the boy went out hunting. He always returned with his catch: geese, ducks, and small sea birds, which he gave to the woman.

As the boy grew older, the man and woman noticed that his face was becoming the color of his copper bow. Wherever he went, there was a strange light. When he sat on the beach looking toward the west, the weather was calm and there were strange bright lights on the water. His foster parents kept wondering about this unusual power, but the boy would not talk about it. When they asked about it, he was always silent.

Once the winds blew so hard over the Great Water that the man could not go out fishing. He had to stay on shore because the ocean waves beat so strongly on the beach. When the father, worried, said they needed to get fish to eat. The boy said, "I will go out fishing with you, for I am stronger than the Spirit of the Storm." The man did not want to go, but at last he listened to the boy. They went out together to the fishing grounds in the rough sea.

They had not gone far when they met the Spirit of the Storm. He tried hard to overturn their boat, but he could not. He had no power over them because the boy was rowing the little boat. All around them the sea was calm and the waves were still.

Then the Spirit of the Storm called his nephew Black Cloud to help him. But the boy said to the man, "Do not be afraid. I am stronger than he." When Black Cloud came, he saw the boy, and he quickly disappeared. Then the Spirit of the Storm called the Mist of the Sea to cover the water, because he thought that the boat would be lost if the land could not be seen.

When the man saw the Mist of the Sea coming across the water, he was very frightened, but the boy said, "He cannot harm you when I am with you." Indeed, when the Mist of the Sea saw the boy sitting in the boat, he went away as quickly as he had come. Angry, the Spirit of the Storm also hurried away. And the sea became calm again.

The boy and the man reached the fishing grounds safely. The boy taught his foster father a magic song, which he could use to call fish into the nets. By evening, the boat was filled with fish. As they were rowing back home, the man said, "Tell me the secret of your power." But the boy said, "The time has not yet come."

The next day the boy killed many birds and took off their skins. Then he dressed himself in the skin of one of the birds and flew above the sea. The sea under him was gray like his wings. Then he dressed himself like another bird, a blue jay. This time, when he flew, the sea under him became blue like his wings. He returned to the beach and put on the skin of a robin redbreast. When he flew high above the sea, the waves in the ocean under him turned the bright color of fire and the sky in the west was a golden red.

The boy flew back to the beach and said to his foster parents, "Now is the time for me to leave you. I am the Child of the Sun. Yesterday my power was tested and I succeeded, so now I must go away. I shall see you no more. But in the evening, I shall often appear to you in the twilight sky in the west. When the sky and the sea are red in the evening, like the color of my face, you will know that there will be no wind or storm the next day. Although I am going away, I shall leave you the power to call me when you need me. Let me know your wishes: make me a white offering, so that I may see it from my home far in the west."

Then he gave his foster mother a wonderful robe. He said good-bye to his parents and flew off to the west. They were left sad and lonely, but the woman still keeps a part of the power he gave her. When she sits on the island and loosens her wonderful robe, the wind blows from the land and a storm begins on the sea. The more she loosens her robe, the stronger the storm is.

In the late autumn, when the cold mist comes from the sea, the evenings are chilly, and the sky is gray, she remembers the boy's promise to her. She takes tiny white feathers from the breasts of birds and throws them into the air. They float to the west and fall to earth like snowflakes that blow westward in the wind. They come to tell the boy the world is gray and gloomy and waiting to see his golden face. Then he appears in the evening and stays until the sun is gone. The twilight sky becomes red and the ocean in the west is filled with golden light. All the people know that there will be no wind the next day, as the boy promised long ago.

Understanding the Story

A. *When Does It Happen?*

Show the order in which the events in the story happen. Write the correct number in the blank.

_____ a. As the boy grows older, the man and woman notice that his face is becoming the color of his copper bow.

_____ b. The foster mother makes an offering of tiny white feathers that fall to earth like snowflakes.

__1__ c. The woman says to herself, "I wish we had children."

_____ d. When the woman opens her robe, the wind blows and a storm begins at sea.

_____ e. The boy flies off to the west.

_____ f. The Spirit of the Storm tries to overturn the boat.

_____ g. The woman finds a baby boy crying on the sand.

_____ h. The boy teaches his foster father a magic song to attract fish.

B. Looking Back

Answer these questions about the story.

1. Why is the woman always so lonely?
2. How does the woman find the baby?
3. As the boy grows bigger, what magical powers does he have?
4. What secret does the boy finally tell his foster parents?
5. What power over nature does the boy give his foster mother?

C. Looking at Two Stories

Complete the chart. Compare "The Boy of the Red Sky" with "The Little Daughter of the Snow" (on pages 11–16).

	"The Boy of the Red Sky"	"The Little Daughter of the Snow"
The couple's feelings at the beginning of the story:		
The couple's feelings after the child arrives:		
What the couple does for the child:		
The reason the child leaves:		

Exploring the Meaning

A. Getting the Deeper Meaning

Discuss these questions about the story.

1. Who are the other characters in the story besides the human characters? What do these characters tell you about how the Native Americans looked at the world?

2. Do you like the ending of the story? Explain your answer.

3. At the end of the story, the couple is once again alone. Give reasons why their lives might have been better if the boy had not come. How might they have been worse?

B. Using Your Imagination

1. Think about what will happen in the future. What will the boy do for his foster parents when they grow old? What will the boy do for the world after he returns to his father, the Sun?

2. Interview the foster parents. Talk to them about life with their special son. Ask:

   - how they felt before the boy came
   - how they felt when the boy was growing up
   - what they thought when the boy showed his magical powers
   - how they felt when the boy left

C. In Everyday Life

Discuss these questions.

1. What joys can children bring to their families? What sorrows can they bring?

2. What tales have you heard that explain happenings in nature such as earthquakes, storms, seasons, or dry or wet weather?

The Spoiled Child

Slavic

Parents in many cultures tell their children about the rewards they will receive if they work hard and are obedient. Parents sometimes even warn their children about the bad things that will happen to them if they don't behave well.

Many folktales tell what happens to lazy children or children who do not obey. This story from Eastern Europe tells about the problems that a spoiled daughter has when she grows up.

Before You Read

Discuss these questions.

1. What is a spoiled child? How might a spoiled child act?
2. Whose fault is it when a child is spoiled?
3. How should children help their parents?

Understanding Key Words

Read the sentences. You will find the words in **bold** in the story. Discuss what each word means.

1. Galinka never carried heavy things. She was not **used to** carrying anything.
2. Galinka's parents never used **harsh** words with her. They did not shout at her and were never angry with her.
3. Galinka did not want to be in the sun. She **complained** that the sun was too hot and would burn her skin.
4. Because Galinka did not water the flowers, they **wilted** and were about to die.
5. When people don't work, they don't **earn** their living.
6. When people work hard all day, they are usually **exhausted** and need to rest.

Words about the Time and Place

You will find these words in the story.

cellar   that part of a house that is underground. It is often a cool place.

cherries   small sweet red fruit

hoe   a tool with a long handle and a piece of metal at the bottom. It is used to turn over the soil and to remove weeds.

spin   to make thread out of cotton or wool by turning and twisting it

thread   a long, thin string of material. Many threads are spun together to make a bigger piece of material.

The Spoiled Child

A husband and wife lived in a village with their only daughter, Galinka. They loved her so much that when she was small they carried her in their arms so that she wouldn't have to walk. They never let her do anything for herself.

Every day, Galinka stayed in bed until late in the morning. Her mother dressed her, combed her hair, and fed her, just like a baby. Then her mother spread a soft rug for her to lie on, left her something nice to eat, and went out to work. All the neighbors said Galinka was spoiled because she was grown up but still did nothing at all, while her mother and father worked hard to give her food and clothes. When it was time for her to get married, young men came to see her, but they all went away again. They all said to themselves, "This is not the wife for a poor, hardworking fellow like me," and they looked for wives in other places.

One day a couple arrived with their only son. He liked Galinka very much and thought that she was the right wife for him. Galinka's mother was willing to give her daughter away in marriage, but she first had plenty to tell the young man's parents.

"My sweet little girl is not used to work, and she must not get tired. You must take care of her well. Don't make her sweep the house and the yard with a broom or the dust will get in her eyes. Don't send her to the well for water. Her shoulders are delicate. She's not used to carrying heavy things. And don't forget to put a nice pillow under her head. Galinka always sleeps on something soft. And promise me you will never shout at Galinka. Her ears are not used to harsh words."

"Don't worry, there are no harsh words in our house," said the bridegroom's father. He got into his cart. His wife got into the front of the cart next to him, and Galinka and her bridegroom got into the back. They traveled to the village where the bridegroom's family lived.

As soon as they arrived home, the mother rolled up her sleeves and set to work to make a large cheese pie. Next she killed a young chicken and boiled it. Then she went down into the cellar to get some wine.

While the bridegroom's mother was doing all that, Galinka was sitting with her arms folded, thinking to herself, "What a good housewife my mother-in-law is! Just like my mother! It will be nice living here."

They all had supper and went to bed.

The next morning the father got up very early and woke up everyone in the family. "Come on, everybody, time to get up!" he shouted. "The sooner we start for the fields the better!"

"What are we going to do there?" asked Galinka, rubbing her sleepy eyes.

"We are going to hoe the corn," said her father-in-law.

"With hoes?" asked the young bride.

"Why, yes, with hoes, of course! What else?" said her mother-in-law.

"Then I'm not coming."

"Not coming? Why not?" asked her bridegroom.

"Because a hoe is too heavy for me!" she answered.

"Leave her alone!" said the old father. "Let her clean up the house and get the supper ready tonight. It's a good idea to leave somebody in the house."

The three of them went into the fields and Galinka was left in the house. She stayed in bed until noon. She got up at noon only because she wanted something to eat. But there was nothing.

"They have left me nothing at all to eat!" she said to herself. "I'll go out in to the garden to have a look at the flowers." Just to stretch her legs, she walked into the garden.

"Oh, what lovely flowers!" she said and she picked a few to smell. Then lying down on the soft grass under a tree, she found cherries hanging above her head. She ate a handful so she wouldn't be hungry. Then yawning from time to time, she passed the day on the grass.

In the evening when the family returned, tired from a hard day's work, what did they find? The house was not clean, the water buckets were not filled, and the fire was not lit. Without saying a word, the old mother brought water, lit the fire, put the potatoes into the pot, and prepared the dough for the bread. She soon had supper ready. Galinka sat on a chair, swinging her legs.

When supper was on the table, the mother called the family. "Come, everybody. Supper is ready!"

Galinka was the first to sit down because she was very hungry. The father broke the bread into three pieces. He handed one piece to his wife, another to his son, and the third he kept for himself.

"And what about the bride?" the mother asked him.

"She is not hungry. If you don't work, you don't get hungry."

Galinka bit her lips and left the table. She went straight to her room and began to cry. She could not sleep. She lay awake all night long thinking how hungry she was.

The next morning the same thing happened. This time the vegetable garden had to be planted. Once more Galinka refused to help.

"The sun is too strong," she complained. "I'll get sunburned."

So they left her at home. Galinka did not think of doing any work. She found a dry piece of bread left for the dog, ate it, and went into the garden to lie on the grass until evening. But now the flowers were wilting in the sun because she hadn't watered them. Later that evening the old parents and their son came home tired out. They found everything just the way they had left it. Once more the mother got the water, lit the fire, prepared the dough, and made the bread. When at last they sat down around the table, the father again broke up the bread into three pieces. Galinka's plate remained empty.

"Why don't you give some bread to the bride?" asked the mother.

"Because a person who likes to eat bread must earn that bread," said the father calmly, and he began to eat.

All night long Galinka turned in her bed, too hungry to sleep.

At dawn, she jumped up and dressed. She looked for everyone, but they had already gone to the fields. Galinka rolled up her sleeves and swept out the house and yard. She carried water from the well. Then she watered the garden, lit the fire, and prepared the supper. She made the dough the way she had seen her mother-in-law do it. She baked the bread. When all the housework was finished, she started to spin the thread. It was hard because she had never made thread before, but she did it.

In the evening, when her young husband and his parents came home exhausted from their day's work and saw what Galinka had done, their eyes lit up. Galinka set the table and gave the bread to her father-in-law. With her heart beating, she waited to see what he would do.

The old man took the bread and broke it into four pieces. The biggest piece he gave to Galinka. He said, "Eat, my child. Now you have earned your bread. You have been working hard today!"

Galinka took the bread and began to eat it. Never in her life had bread tasted so sweet.

Understanding the Story

A. What Happens?

Match the sentence parts. Write the correct letter in each blank.

_____ 1. Galinka's parents do not let her

_____ 2. Many young men come to see Galinka

_____ 3. Galinka's mother tells

_____ 4. Galinka's mother-in-law works

_____ 5. When her husband's family goes to work in the fields, Galinka

_____ 6. Galinka's father-in-law gives

_____ 7. On the third day, Galinka

_____ 8. When Galinka works,

a. her no bread because she does not work.

b. stays home and does nothing.

c. she receives a large piece of the bread.

d. but do not want to marry her.

e. the young man's parents not to make her work.

f. prepares the supper.

g. do any work.

h. in the house and in the fields.

B. Looking Back

Answer these questions about the story.

1. Why don't Galinka's parents give her any work to do?

2. Why do many men decide not to marry Galinka?

3. How does Galinka's mother want her new husband's family to treat Galinka?

4. What does her husband's family think Galinka should do?

5. How does Galinka's father-in-law change Galinka's habits?

6. How does Galinka surprise the family?

C. Understanding Characters' Actions and Feelings

Complete the chart. Write what Galinka does at different times in the story. Then use these words or other words that you know to tell how she feels:

bored   happy   hungry   proud   sad   satisfied   upset

When in the Story	What Galinka Does	How Galinka Feels
The evening she arrives at her husband's house:	*She watches her mother-in-law make supper.*	*Satisfied, pleased, happy*
During the first day:		
The first evening after supper:		
During the second day:		
The second evening after supper:		
During the third day:		
The third evening at supper:		

Exploring the Meaning

A. Getting the Deeper Meaning

Answer these questions about the story.

1. Is it Galinka's fault that she is so lazy? Why or why not?
2. Why isn't Galinka really a part of the family when she first arrives at her husband's house?
3. What does she learn about work and helping others?
4. Do you know any stories in which people are rewarded for working hard? Do you know any stories in which people are punished for not working hard?

B. Survey

In the story, the people do work and chores. Make a list of common chores, such as doing laundry, cooking, and washing dishes.

Then, using your list, do a survey of your class and other people you know. Ask: "What chores do you usually do? What chores don't you like to do?"

Write the results of the surveys. Which chores do most people do? What chores don't people like to do? Share your results with the class.

C. In Everyday Life

Discuss these questions.

1. How do you think children should be raised so they are ready for adult responsibilities?
2. Why do parents spoil children?
3. In the story, the women do the work in the house. Does this vary from culture to culture? Do you think one person should do all the housework? Should the housework be shared?

Challenge and Adventure

The Fisherman and the Genie

Arab

The Arabian Nights, *also known as* The Thousand and One Nights, *includes the adventures of famous characters such as Aladdin, Ali Baba, and Sinbad. These stories are from Arabia, Egypt, India, Iran, and other countries in Asia and the Middle East. Some of them are more than a thousand years old. The fisherman in this story from the* Arabian Nights *has a real challenge: he is in danger of losing his life. Read about how he meets the challenge.*

Before You Read

Talk about the following.

1. Many people fish to earn their living. What kinds of problems can these people have?

2. Have you ever gone fishing? Was it fun?

3. Share with your class stories such as "Ali Baba and the Forty Thieves" and "Aladdin and the Magic Lamp" that you know from the *Arabian Nights.*

Understanding Key Words

Read the sentences. You will find the words in **bold** in the story. Discuss what each word means.

1. The fisherman was so poor that he could **barely support** his family. They had almost no money to buy food or anything else.

2. The fisherman had trouble pulling the heavy net out of the water. He felt a great **weight** in it.

3. The fisherman needed to catch fish. But he saw that he had caught only a basket of trash. He felt sad and **miserable.**

4. The vase was **sealed.** It was closed tightly so that nothing could come out.

5. The smoke **spread** in the sky. It moved slowly and filled the sky.

6. At first, the genie **vowed** to help anyone who freed him. Later, he decided not to keep the promise.

7. The genie was angry because nobody had **released** him for so long. No one had freed him from the bottle for hundreds of years.

Words about the Time and Place

Here are some special words from the *Arabian Nights* story. You will find these words in the story.

genie   an imaginary character who has magical powers

fortune   luck, chance. In the story, Fortune is the power that decides what good or bad things happen to a person.

treasure   riches. They can include money, jewelry, and gold.

The Fisherman and the Genie

Once upon a time, there was a fisherman who was so old and poor that he could barely support his wife and three children. Every day he went fishing very early, but he never threw his nets into the sea more than four times.

One morning he started out by moonlight and came to the seashore. He threw his nets into the sea. As he was pulling them back toward the shore, he felt a great weight. He thought he had caught a large fish, and so he felt very happy. But a moment later he saw that he had no fish, rather only a dead donkey. He was very disappointed.

Then the fisherman became angry. He had just repaired his nets, and he noticed that the weight of the dead donkey had broken them in several places. Still he threw the nets into the sea a second time. When he drew them in, he felt a great weight, and so again he thought they were full of fish. But he found only a large basket full of trash. He felt even more miserable.

"O Fortune," he cried. "Do not play games with me, a poor fisherman who can hardly support his family." After he had washed his nets, he threw them into the sea for the third time. But this time he drew in only stones, shells, and mud. He almost gave up hope of getting a fish.

Then he threw his nets into the sea a fourth time. This time he thought he had a fish, but again there was no fish, rather only a copper vase. From its weight, the vase seemed to be full of something. He noticed that it was closed and sealed with lead. He was very excited and decided to sell the vase. With the money, he planned to buy wheat.

He examined the vase and shook it. Although he heard nothing, he thought there must be something valuable inside the vase because it was sealed. With his knife, he opened it. He turned it upside down, but nothing came out. While he was looking at it in disappointment,

a thick smoke came out of the vase. The smoke rose up in a cloud that stretched over the sea and the shore. When all the smoke was out of the vase, a genie formed, twice as large as the largest giant. When the fisherman saw such a terrible-looking monster, he was so frightened he could not move.

"Great king of the genies," called the monster, "I will never again disobey you!"

Hearing those words, the fisherman became brave and said, "Tell me why you were locked up in the vase."

The giant looked at the fisherman and said, "Speak to me more politely or I shall kill you."

"Why should you kill me?" asked the fisherman. "I have just freed you. Have you forgotten that?"

"No," answered the genie, "but that will not stop me from killing you. I am only going to do you one favor: you may choose the way you will die. I cannot treat you in any other way. If you want to know why, listen to my story."

"I fought against the king of the genies. To punish me, he shut me up in this copper vase and put his lead seal on it to keep me from coming out. Then he had the vase thrown into the sea. I made a vow that if anyone freed me before a hundred years had passed, I would make him rich even after his death. But nobody freed me. I made a vow that if anyone freed me in the second century, I would give him all the treasures in the world. But nobody freed me. In the third century, I promised to make him king, always to be near him, and grant him three wishes every day. But nobody freed me. At last, I grew angry at being kept in the vase so long and vowed that if anyone released me, I would kill him at once and would only allow him to choose the way he would die. So you may choose the way you will die."

The fisherman was very sad. "What an unlucky man I am for freeing you. Please do not kill me."

"I have told you," said the genie, "that is impossible. Quickly, choose how you will die."

The fisherman began to think of a way to trick the genie.

"I really cannot believe," said the fisherman, "that this vase can hold your feet and even your whole body. I cannot believe it unless you show me."

The genie began to change himself into smoke, which spread over the sea and the shore. Collecting itself together, the smoke began to go back into the vase until there was nothing left outside. Then a voice came from inside the vase. It said to the fisherman, "Well, unbelieving fisherman, here I am in the vase. Do you believe me now?"

Instead of answering, the fisherman quickly took the lead lid and shut the top of the vase.

"Now, Genie, you will ask me to pardon you!" shouted the fisherman. "And I will choose how you die! But no, it is better if I throw you into the sea. And I will build a house on the shore to warn other fishermen who cast their nets here. And so they will know not to fish up an evil genie like you."

When he heard those words, the genie did everything he could to get out of the vase. But he could not, because the lid was tightly shut.

Then he tried to get out with a clever trick.

"If you take off the lid, I will repay you," said the genie.

"No," answered the fisherman, and he threw the vase far out into the sea.

Understanding the Story

A. What Happens?

Complete each sentence by choosing **a, b, c,** or **d.**

1. The first time the fisherman throws his nets into the sea he catches
   a. a large fish. c. a sealed vase.
   b. a dead donkey. d. a basket of trash.

2. When the fisherman opens the vase, the first thing that comes out is
   a. stones, shells, and mud. c. a strange smell.
   b. a terrible genie. d. a thick smoke.

3. At first, the genie is in the vase because
    a. he wanted to see if he could fit into it.
    b. he fought the king of the genies.
    c. he needed to hide from the king of the genies.
    d. the fisherman put him there.

4. The genie tells the fisherman that
    a. he will let him choose the way he wants to die.
    b. he will make him rich even after his death.
    c. he will give him all the treasures in the world.
    d. he will grant him three wishes a day.

5. The fisherman saves his own life by
    a. agreeing to the genie's wishes.
    b. begging the genie to let him live.
    c. tricking the genie to go back into the vase.
    d. pushing the genie back into the vase.

B. Looking Back

Answer these questions about the story.

1. Why does the fisherman throw his net out four times?
2. Why is the fisherman happy when he finds a vase in the net?
3. Why is the vase sealed?
4. Why does the genie want to kill the fisherman who freed him?
5. Why does the genie go back into the vase?
6. Why does the fisherman want to build a house?

C. Understanding Characters' Feelings

Complete the chart on page 45. Tell how the fisherman feels at different times in the story and the reasons why. Use these words and other words that you know:

afraid angry brave disappointed
excited hopeless miserable sad

When?	How the Fisherman Feels	Reason
The first time he throws his nets into the sea	*disappointed*	*He finds a dead donkey in his net.*
The second time he throws his nets into the sea:		
The third time he throws his nets into the sea:		
When he finds the vase:		
When the genie says, "Great king of the genies":		
When the genie says, "You must choose how you want to die":		
When the genie goes back into the vase:		

Exploring the Meaning

A. *Getting the Deeper Meaning*

Discuss these questions about the story.

1. A reader may have one opinion of the fisherman at the beginning of the story, but a different opinion at the end. Why might the reader's opinion about the fisherman change?
2. Why is the genie unfair to the fisherman who frees him?
3. Do you think that the story has a "happy ending"?
4. How does the fisherman's life prepare him to face the genie cleverly?

B. *Survey*

The genie says that he had made a promise: He is going to give three wishes to the person who frees him. Do a survey. Ask five people, "If you had three wishes, what would you wish?" Write the results of the survey. Share your results with the class. What wishes are the most popular? What wishes are the most interesting?

C. *In Everyday Life*

Discuss the following.

1. The fisherman calls on Fortune when he has bad luck. Do you believe that you can make your own luck?
2. The fisherman has to think quickly to save his own life. Tell about a time when you had to quickly solve a problem.
3. This story is very well known. Why do you think people like this story?
4. The fisherman accidently finds the vase and releases an evil genie. Can you think of any "evil genies" that have been released in the modern world?

The Woodsman's Daughter and the Lion

Puerto Rican

Cultures throughout the world tell tales in which animals play important roles. This tale from Puerto Rico, an island in the Caribbean, tells about a brave young girl and a lion. If you know the story of "Beauty and the Beast," you will recognize parts of this story.

Before You Read

Discuss these questions.

1. What does a woodsman do in the forest?
2. What words would you use to describe a lion?
3. Do you know any tales in which an animal changes into a human being? If so, share one with the class.

Understanding Key Words

Read the sentences. You will find words in **bold** in the story. Discuss what each word means.

1. The woodsman asked the lion again and again not to eat him. He **begged** the lion to let him live.
2. The man made an **agreement** with the lion. He promised to do something if the lion let him live.
3. The daughter felt sad because she couldn't see her family. She **missed** them very much.
4. The door of the cave was **sealed up.** No one could get in or out of the cave.
5. The young woman walked everywhere, trying to find the lion. She **went in search of** him throughout the world.
6. In **desperation**, the young woman continued to knock on the door. She was losing hope of getting in, but she did not know what else to do.
7. The young woman kept thinking about the lion and trying to find him. She showed her **loyalty** to the lion.

Words about the Time and Place

You will find these words in the story.

blacksmith	a person who makes things in iron. This person's job includes putting iron shoes on horses.
carriage	an elegant wagon, pulled by horses, in which people travel
enchanted	something that is under the power of magic
palace	an elegant house, usually for a king or queen
rooster	a male chicken. A rooster crows in the morning, making loud, unpleasant noises.
spell	magic words that make something happen

The Woodsman's Daughter and the Lion

There was once a woodsman who went to the forest every day to cut wood. One day while he was chopping down a tree, a great, fierce lion appeared. Fearing for his life, the woodsman threw himself on the ground and begged the lion not to eat him. He explained that he was a poor woodsman who had to work hard to take care of his three daughters.

When the lion heard this, he said, "Very well, I shall not eat you, but you must make me a promise." The woodsman was pleased with this suggestion, so he agreed to promise to do whatever the lion asked.

The lion said, "I will not eat you if you promise to bring me, tomorrow, the first thing that comes to greet you when you get home this afternoon."

The woodsman was even more pleased at this. He thought how easily he had saved his life, because it was his little dog that always ran out to greet him. So he made the promise.

That afternoon the woodsman collected the wood he had cut and set off for home, feeling very lucky. But happiness soon changed to sorrow. The little dog that usually ran up to him when he got near home did not greet him. Instead his youngest daughter ran out. She threw her arms around her father. She told her father that the dog was inside because he had a thorn in his paw.

When he went in to the house, his daughters noticed their father's sadness. They asked him what had happened to make him so unhappy. Crying, the woodsman told them about his promise to the lion and how he had to take the youngest daughter to the lion tomorrow. He loved his daughter very much, but he had to keep his word. He didn't know what to do!

The youngest daughter, who loved her father more than the other two did, told him not to worry. She said that she wasn't afraid to go with him tomorrow to meet the lion.

The next morning the woodsman and his daughter set out to meet the lion. When they reached the place in the forest where the lion had appeared the day before, there he was, waiting for them. The woodsman begged the lion to free him from the agreement. He said that he loved his daughter so much that he could not bear to lose her. The lion refused and said to the girl, "Follow me." But before leaving, he told the woodsman to dig under a nearby tree and he would find gold at its roots. Then the lion entered a cave, and the young girl followed him, leaving her father alone in tears.

After they had gone, the woodsman remembered what the lion had told him. He dug under the tree and found many gold coins. He took them home. With so much money, he and his daughters lived without having to work so hard.

Meanwhile, the youngest daughter had come with the lion to an underground palace. There she found many beautiful dresses, jewelry, and all the lovely things she had dreamed about. The lion was very kind and gave her anything she asked for.

Months passed, and the young girl grew very unhappy because she missed her family. One day the lion asked her why she was so sad. She told him that she was sad because she had not seen her sisters or her father for such a long time. The lion told her that the next day she could visit them, but that she must return before the rooster crowed at sunrise. This made her happy again.

The next morning, when she left the cave, there was a carriage waiting to take her to her father's house. At home, everyone was pleased to hear how well she was living and how kind the lion was to her. Before the rooster crowed at sunrise, the young girl said good-bye to her father and sisters and stepped into the carriage to return to the enchanted palace.

Months passed, and again the girl grew sad, so the lion told her to visit her home once more, and reminded her to return before the rooster crowed. Happily, she stepped into the carriage to go to her father's house. When she arrived, she found that her father was ill. She gave him his medicine and cared for him. But she was so busy with his illness she did not notice that the sun had risen and the roosters were crowing to announce a new day.

When she realized what had happened, she was frightened. She said good-bye to her father and her sisters and hurried out to the carriage that had brought her. It was gone! Very upset about having broken her promise to the lion, she walked to the woods and came to the tree where she had first met him. There was nothing there. She continued walking and came to the entrance of the cave, but it was sealed up. She sat down and cried. As she sat there, she heard the voice of the lion telling her that he was actually a prince who was under a magic spell. She had *almost* broken this spell. But now she would have to walk across the world and wear out a pair of iron shoes before she could find him again to break the spell and set him free.

Through her tears, the girl promised that she would do this. She went to the blacksmith and had him make her a pair of iron shoes. She put them on and began walking across the world in search of the lion.

She spent many years searching for him. When the iron soles of her shoes were worn as thin as a sheet of paper, she reached the house of the Sun. The Sun said he didn't know where the enchanted lion was but that perhaps the Moon would know. When the young girl arrived at the Moon's house, the Moon said she had seen him at night in a castle behind the great mountain. The young girl left for the great mountain.

After walking across the mountain, she came to a castle with

large, locked doors. She knocked and knocked at one of the doors, but no one opened it. In desperation, she pulled off one of her iron shoes and threw it at the door. Instantly, all the doors flew open. As though by magic, a handsome prince appeared and took her in his arms. He explained that he had been the lion. Thanks to her love and loyalty, he had been freed from the evil spell that was cast upon him.

The young girl was filled with joy and lived happily with the prince. Her father and sisters also came to live with them.

Understanding the Story

A. When Does It Happen?

Show the order in which the events in the story happen. Write the correct number in the blank.

_____ a. When she throws her shoe at the door, a prince comes out.

_____ b. The daughter finds beautiful clothes and jewelry in the palace.

_____ c. When the daughter comes out late, the carriage is gone.

_____ d. The woodsman digs under the tree and finds gold.

_____ e. The daughter walks across the world in iron shoes.

_1_ f. The lion agrees not to eat the woodsman.

_____ g. The lion allows the daughter to visit her family.

_____ h. The daughter goes in the woods with the lion.

B. Looking Back

Answer these questions about the story.

1. Why does the woodsman's daughter have to go with the lion?
2. How does the lion treat the woodsman's daughter?
3. Before the lion lets the daughter visit her family, what does he tell her?
4. Why does the daughter have to walk across the world in iron shoes?
5. Why does the lion turn into a prince?

C. *Understanding the Characters' Problems*

Complete the chart. Write the problems.

Character	Problem
The Woodsman 1. The problem at the beginning of the story, when he first meets the lion: 2. The problem he has when his daughter, not his dog, comes to greet him:	1. 2.
The Woodsman's Daughter 1. The problem she has after living with the lion for several months: 2. The problem she has when she returns late to the lion's cave: 3. The problem she has when she arrives at the castle where the lion is:	1. 2. 3.
The Lion The problem he has until the very end of the story:	

Exploring the Meaning

A. *Getting the Deeper Meaning*

Discuss these questions about the story.

1. Why is the daughter the heroine of this story?
2. Do you think that it is fair or unfair that the lion is freed from the magical spell only *after* the woodsman's daughter shows courage and loyalty?
3. What does this story say about making agreements and keeping promises?

B. *Your Ideas about the Character*

The woodsman's daughter is the heroine of this tale. Work with a partner to choose the one word or phrase that you think best describes her. List three reasons why you think your choice best describes the woodsman's daughter. Give examples from the story. Share your ideas with the class.

- loyal
- afraid
- caring

- brave
- patient
- keeps trying, does not give up

C. *In Everyday Life*

Discuss these questions.

1. When should people keep promises and when should they break them?
2. How do children help their parents in your native culture?

The Lucky Charm

Guatemalan

Guatemala is a small country in Central America, south of Mexico. It was home to one of the great civilizations of the world, the Mayan. This story comes from one of the Native American tribes or groups who live in the area.

The themes in "The Lucky Charm" are common to many folktales.

"The Lucky Charm"

- *tells of a brave young hero.*
- *has a main character with unusual powers.*
- *explains the origin of something in nature.*

Before You Read

Discuss these questions.

1. Why do people wear or carry lucky charms?
2. What kinds of charms do people you know wear or carry?
3. What do you know about the Mayan Indians who lived in Central America?

Understanding Key Words

Read the sentences. You will find the words in **bold** in the story. Discuss what each word means.

1. The wise man **predicted** that Quetzal would have an unusual future.

2. When Quetzal's father died, many people **offered consolation** to Quetzal. They let him know how sad they were that his father had died.

3. There was a **mourning** period after the death of the old chief. During that time, the people in the tribe remembered and honored their chief.

4. The wise men **announced** the name of the new chief. They told the name to the entire tribe.

5. The young man was **in a panic** when he found that his lucky charm was gone. He was so upset that he didn't know what to do.

6. The enemies **aimed** their arrows at Quetzal. They pointed their arrows at him.

Words about the Time and Place

You will find these words in the story.

bow and arrow	An arrow is a stick with a sharp tip. It is shot from a bow, a curved strip of wood.
council	the group that makes decisions for the tribe
fortune-teller	a person who is believed to be able to predict the future
hummingbird	a very tiny bird with a long, narrow beak
soothsayer	a person who is believed to be able to tell what will happen in the future

---

The Lucky Charm

Except for the chief, the most important person in the Quiché tribe was the soothsayer. The soothsayer was really a fortune-teller. He could tell what was going to happen in the future. Everyone believed that the gods spoke to the soothsayer, so no one questioned his words. The chief and the wise men of the Quiché tribe listened to what he had to say before they made a decision.

Many years ago a son was born to the chief of the Quiché tribe. He named the baby Quetzal.

There was a great celebration. When the soothsayer began to speak, everyone listened with respect, fear, and wonder.

"This young man," the soothsayer began, "will be loved and admired by the tribe. His future is most unusual. I cannot reveal that secret until the time is right. Only when Quetzal grows up, will I tell you what the future holds in store for him."

As time passed, Quetzal became everything the soothsayer had predicted. He was an excellent hunter and fisherman, and he showed great strength and courage. Even when he was still a child, he had the wisdom and understanding of a grown man.

The years passed quickly and soon Quetzal would be an adult who could take part in the council meetings with his father, the wise men, and the soothsayer.

One morning Quetzal came to call his father to a meeting. He was shocked to discover that the old chief had died quietly and peacefully in his sleep. Everyone in the tribe was saddened and tried to offer consolation to the young son. The wise men announced that the new chief was Quetzal.

When the mourning period ended, the tribe began to prepare for the celebration to honor the new leader. Musicians wore purple and dark red robes and played many musical instruments. There was dancing and a great feast that lasted throughout the night.

As the light of day appeared in the sky, the tribe became silent, awaiting the words of the soothsayer. He held his hands up high. On one of his wrists hung a necklace: it was a good-luck charm. After praying to the gods, the soothsayer placed the necklace around Quetzal's neck.

Then the soothsayer spoke. "Quetzal is now a man and our chief. When he was born, I told you there was a secret I could not reveal until the time was right. Now that he is a man, I can tell you. His future is protected forever by the gods. They have decided that Quetzal will never die. He will live forever through all time."

The people shouted joyfully and thanked the gods. They all fell to their knees in front of Quetzal, whom the gods had chosen to honor. Only one person did not bow down: Chiruma, Quetzal's evil uncle. He quietly left to think about the meaning of the soothsayer's words.

Now, Chiruma was only a few years older than Quetzal, his nephew. He had hoped that Quetzal's life would be short so that he could become chief. But how could his dream come true if Quetzal would live forever?

Chiruma sat with his face in his hands and began to plan how to end the life of his nephew.

Suddenly the alarm sounded, warning the Quiché warriors that a neighboring tribe was attacking them during the celebration.

Although this was Quetzal's first chance to fight, he fought bravely. The battle was short. Quetzal was in front, leading the warriors. Each time the enemy aimed an arrow in the direction of Quetzal, it fell to the ground. Finally the enemy fled because they thought that magic made the arrows turn aside and fall without harming anyone.

But Chiruma knew better. He was sure that Quetzal was protected by the charm the soothsayer had placed around his neck. So the evil uncle decided to steal the magical charm.

That night Chiruma came quietly into the room where Quetzal lay sound asleep. Without waking him, Chiruma lifted his nephew's blanket and saw the tiny feather of a hummingbird hanging from the charm around his neck. Chiruma quietly lifted his knife and cut the deerskin cord on which the feather hung. Then holding the necklace tightly in his hand, he quietly left the room.

"This is a powerful charm," said Chiruma to himself joyfully. "Now we shall see if Quetzal will live forever."

The next morning Quetzal discovered the necklace with the feather was gone. He was in a panic. He ran silently into the forest where the soothsayer lived. Quetzal was sure that the soothsayer could help him. Unfortunately Quetzal was being followed by the evil Chiruma. Taking a shortcut through the forest, the evil uncle reached the soothsayer's house before Quetzal. There he hid behind a tree, holding his bow and arrow.

When Quetzal was a short distance from the soothsayer's house, he heard the sound of the wings of many hummingbirds. But the warning came too late. An arrow flew through the air and struck his chest.

The soothsayer heard the noise outside, but he was too late to save Quetzal. When he saw the cruel uncle run through the forest, he shouted to him, "You have stolen the lucky charm, but its magic belongs only to Quetzal. It will not protect you."

But Chiruma did not hear these words because he was in a hurry to get back to the village. He told everyone there that one of the enemy had killed the new chief.

The soothsayer, on hearing what Chiruma had said, remained

silent because he knew that the gods would have their own way of punishing Chiruma.

The gods kept their promise to Quetzal. They changed him into a beautiful bird that still lives in the forests of Guatemala. Its body is green like the grass on which Quetzal lay as he died. Its breast is the color of blood. Its blue-green tail is three to six feet long and hangs down from the branches as the bird sits in trees.

Before the soothsayer died, he told everyone of the origin of the quetzal bird, from the warrior Quetzal. The bird has always been considered holy in Guatemala and cannot be hunted. It is on the national coat of arms of Guatemala, as well as on its coins, which are called quetzals. So the young chief does indeed live forever.

Understanding the Story

A. What Happens?

Complete each sentence by choosing **a, b,** or **c.**

1. When Quetzal is growing up, he
    a. makes predictions.
    b. shows great strength and courage.
    c. fights in many battles.

2. At the celebration when Quetzal becomes the chief of the tribe,
    a. the soothsayer makes an unusual prediction.
    b. Quetzal tells about his unusual future.
    c. Chiruma shows great respect for Quetzal.

3. Chiruma decides to
    a. kill Quetzal and then steal the lucky charm.
    b. steal the lucky charm and then kill Quetzal in the forest.
    c. steal the lucky charm, so the enemy's arrows could kill Quetzal.

4. The evil uncle
    a. runs away and is never seen again.
    b. tells everyone he has killed Quetzal.
    c. tells everyone the enemy has killed Quetzal.

5. The quetzal bird has
   a. a green body like the grass on which Quetzal died.
   b. a green body like the color of the charm Quetzal wore.
   c. a red body like the color of Quetzal's blood.

B. Looking Back

Discuss these questions about the story.

1. Why does everyone in the tribe listen to the soothsayer?
2. When Quetzal is growing up, what kind of person is he?
3. Why does Chiruma kill Quetzal?
4. What happens to arrows that are shot at Quetzal before the lucky charm is stolen? What happens to the arrow that is shot at Quetzal after the lucky charm is stolen?
5. How does Quetzal live forever?

C. Understanding the Parts of the Story

Complete the chart. Tell what prediction the soothsayer makes at each point in the story. Tell if the prediction comes true.

When the Prediction is made	What Does the Soothsayer Predict?	Does the Prediction Come True?
At Quetzal's birth		
At the celebration when Quetzal becomes the chief		
After Chiruma kills Quetzal		

Exploring the Meaning

A. Getting the Deeper Meaning

Discuss these questions about the story.

1. When the soothsayer gives his prediction about Quetzal at the cele-bration, the people think they understand his future, but they are wrong. What do they think will happen? What really happens?

2. Is the soothsayer right or wrong not to tell the people what he knows about Chiruma?

3. What does this story say about jealousy?

B. Telling the Story Again

Imagine that you are a member of the Quiché tribe. Tell the story of Quetzal to younger members of the tribe. Tell:

- what Quetzal was like
- what happened the night of the celebration when Quetzal be-came chief
- what happened the day Quetzal was killed
- the story of the quetzal bird

C. In Everyday Life

Discuss the following.

1. Do you think that famous people live forever? Give examples.

2. Why do people want to live forever?

3. Give any examples you know of crimes people have committed be-cause of jealousy.

4. Do you think that it is a good idea to carry a lucky charm?

Nazar the Brave

Armenian

Armenia is a small country in western Asia. It has been conquered many times in its long history. Today about half of the Armenians live outside their country but still try to keep their culture and language alive.

The story that you are going to read is amusing. It tells about a coward who people think is brave. You'll find out about the many adventures of this "hero."

Before You Read

Discuss these questions.

1. When would you call a person "brave"?
2. What are some jobs that require people to act bravely? Would you like to have one of these jobs?
3. Are there people in your town or neighborhood who you think are brave? Tell about them.

Understanding Key Words

Read the sentences. You will find the words in **bold** in the story. Discuss what each word means.

1. Nazar was a **coward.** He was afraid of everything and everyone. He was not **courageous.**

2. Nazar was afraid of the dark. He did not **dare** go outside at night.

3. Nazar often made **boasts.** He said he could do anything.

4. Nazar wanted his wife to **rescue** him from the bad situation, but she would not save him.

5. The wedding guests were **impressed** by Nazar. They thought he was a great man.

6. Some of the guests **pretended** they knew Nazar. They said that they had met him, but this wasn't true.

7. The tiger **terrified** the village people. They were so frightened that they wanted the tiger killed as soon as possible.

Words about the Time and Place

You will find these words in the story.

banner	a flag
caravan	a group of people traveling together through a dangerous place to somewhere safer
club	a heavy stick, usually with a round end
giant	a very big, strong person, often found in folktales
sword	a very long knife used to fight in battles
toast	a short speech to honor someone, said before drinking

Nazar the Brave

Once there was and was not a simple man in Armenia named Nazar, who was both lazy and stupid. Worse than that, he was a terrible coward. He was afraid of everything: of the light, of the dark, of the day, and of the night. He did not dare take a step by himself. He hung on to his wife's apron strings from morning till night, following the poor woman wherever she went. So people called him Nazar the Fearful.

One night Nazar said to his wife, "What a wonderful night for a robbery! My heart tells me to go and rob the caravan of the rich shah who visits our land from India. Why won't you let me rob him? Am I not a man? Why do you stop me?"

Sick of her husband's empty boasts, Nazar's wife called out, "All right. Go ahead and rob the shah's caravan. And don't come back here till you do!" And she locked him out of the house.

Poor Nazar was frightened. He begged his wife to rescue him, but she wouldn't listen. Tired, he finally fell asleep outside the house.

It was a hot, sticky night. Thousands of flies buzzed over Nazar's face, sticking to his nose and lips. Without opening his eyes, he angrily raised his hand and slapped at the flies. Dead flies fell all around him. Nazar opened his eyes and saw the dead flies on the ground.

He began to count the number of flies he had killed at one blow. There were so many that he lost count.

"Ah! What a brave man I am! I never knew it until today! I can kill a thousand living things at one blow, but I have been waiting hand and foot on my ungrateful wife."

He went off to the village priest and told him the story of his bravery. He begged the priest to write about his courageous act so that everyone would know about it.

Laughing, the good-natured priest took a piece of cloth and jokingly wrote in large letters:

NAZAR THE BRAVE, OUR MIGHTY HERO, FELLS A THOUSAND AT A SINGLE BLOW.

Nazar attached the cloth to the end of a long pole to make a banner, put a rusty sword into his belt, got on his neighbor's donkey, and rode out of the village into the forest.

As he left his home farther and farther behind him, Nazar became more and more frightened. To keep up his spirits, he began to talk to himself and to shout at the donkey. The poor donkey brayed louder and louder as Nazar shouted louder and louder.

A simple man heard all the noise and shouting. "It must be thieves!" he thought. Leaving his horse in the forest, the man fled for his life.

When Nazar approached the spot, he saw a horse with an expensive saddle. Getting off his donkey, he got on the horse and continued on his way.

Finally, he reached a village where a wedding feast was in progress. "Good day," said Nazar as he rode toward the wedding guests. They answered, "Come and join us." The villagers took Nazar with his banner to the head of the table and offered him food and drink. They were curious about this stranger, but they were simple people who could not read. Each whispered, "Who is he?" Finally the question reached the village priest, who read the banner to himself and to the people sitting near him who repeated it to their neighbors until all the wedding guests knew who Nazar was:

NAZAR THE BRAVE, OUR MIGHTY HERO, FELLS A THOUSAND AT A SINGLE BLOW.

Several guests pretended to have heard of him and began to whisper that they knew of Nazar's past bravery. Some of the guests wondered why he had no servant. Others wondered why such a brave man did not carry a real sword, only a small rusty one. The guests were very impressed with their visitor. They drank many toasts in his honor.

When the wedding celebration ended, Nazar rode away from the village, trembling with fear at the darkness and the strange, unfamiliar roads. Finally, he reached an open green field. Frightened, he got off his horse and managed to fall asleep.

The field belonged to seven giants who lived in a castle on top of the mountain next to the open space. In the morning, the giants looked out and saw that someone had dared to trespass on their land. Angrily, they put their clubs on their shoulders and came down to the field. They found Nazar asleep under the banner that read:

NAZAR THE BRAVE, OUR MIGHTY HERO,
FELLS A THOUSAND AT A SINGLE BLOW.

"It's Nazar the Brave!" exclaimed the giants. "The hero we have heard so much about from all the villagers." They looked fearfully at the man who could kill a thousand at a single blow.

Suddenly, Nazar awoke. When he opened his eyes and saw seven giants armed with clubs towering over him, his stomach turned over! Trembling like a fall leaf, he tried to crawl under his banner.

When the giants saw him turn purple and tremble, they were frightened. "Nazar the Brave is angry. Now he will kill us at one blow!" They fell upon their knees and begged him not to kill them. "O Nazar the Brave, we have heard of your fame. Come to our home on the hill." And Nazar allowed them to take him to their castle, where he was an honored guest.

At that time, a man-eating tiger suddenly appeared in the country-side, terrifying the people. They agreed that the tiger must be killed, but who was brave enough to try? "Nazar the Brave, of course!" exclaimed the villagers, and they came to Nazar for help.

As soon as Nazar heard the word *tiger,* he began to shake with fright and ran out of the castle to go back to his own village and his wife. But the people thought that he was running to kill the tiger.

One shouted, "Take this knife with you!" Grabbing it, Nazar ran into the forest as fast as he could go and climbed to the top of the tallest tree he could find. Scared to death, he held on, hoping never to see the tiger.

As luck would have it, the tiger chose to walk through the forest and decided to lie down under that same tree!

Nazar looked down and saw the tiger. He trembled so much that he lost his hold on the tree. Down he fell, right onto the back of the tiger! Up it jumped, trying to shake off the strange weight on its

back. Roaring wildly, the tiger ran out of the forest, while Nazar, shaking with fear, hung on.

"Look!" shouted the people waiting outside the village. "Nazar has tamed the tiger and is riding it like a horse!" Nazar's bravery gave them courage, and so the villagers surrounded the tiger and killed it. Nazar shouted to the villagers, "Why did you kill the animal? I was going to keep it for a horse!"

News of this bravery spread throughout the countryside. All the people turned out to welcome Nazar and to honor him.

Some weeks later, the giants learned that a neighboring king was coming to attack them. They came to ask Nazar for help, and they put him in command of their army.

When war was mentioned, Nazar quaked with fear. Again he started to run out of the castle back to his own village.

News of Nazar's courage had spread throughout the giants' army. The soldiers wanted to follow such a daring commander.

When the soldiers saw Nazar running, they thought that he was rushing off to fight the enemy. The soldiers helped Nazar get on a horse. Everyone waited for his command, but Nazar's horse, sensing that the rider had no control, bolted straight ahead toward the enemy camp. Nazar's soldiers thought that their commander was leading an attack, so they galloped after him.

The frightened Nazar realized that his horse was leading him right into the territory of the enemy, so he decided to save himself by jumping off the horse into a tree along the way. He grabbed for a branch, which broke off. Nazar was now holding a large part of the tree and was still on the horse.

When the enemy saw the famed hero, Nazar, galloping toward them with a tree in his hand, they shouted, "Run for your lives! Nazar the Brave is coming to kill us, and he's tearing up the trees as he comes!" Many of the enemy were killed in the battle that followed. The survivors surrendered to Nazar.

What a ceremony welcomed Nazar back to the giants' castle! He became king of the land. The people gave him gifts and honors. The seven giants became his advisors. And he ruled wisely and well forever after.

Understanding the Story

A. What Happens?

Complete each sentence by choosing **a, b,** or **c.**

1. When Nazar tells his wife he wants to rob the shah's caravan, she
   a. tells him he will be killed.
   b. says she will help him.
   c. tells him to go ahead and do it.

2. After Nazar kills all the flies, he
   a. goes to sleep.
   b. tells his wife about his bravery.
   c. goes to the priest so his story can be written down.

3. At the wedding feast, the people
   a. believe that Nazar is a brave man.
   b. ignore Nazar.
   c. ask Nazar to fight the tiger.

4. When Nazar hears about the tiger, he
   a. chases it around the forest.
   b. runs away as fast as he can.
   c. jumps on it and tries to kill it.

5. The enemy gives in to Nazar and his army because
   a. they are terrified when they see him coming with a tree in his hand.
   b. they hear he has tamed a tiger.
   c. he comes galloping toward them with the giants at his side.

B. Looking Back

Answer these questions about the story.

1. What is Nazar like?
2. How does Nazar's wife feel about him?
3. Why does the village priest write a joke on Nazar's banner?
4. How does Nazar act every time he hears about danger?
5. Why are the giants important in this story?
6. How is Nazar rewarded for his "bravery"?

C. Understanding a Character's Actions

Complete the chart to show what people think about Nazar.

Action	What People Think Nazar Is Doing or Had Done
Nazar carries a banner that says he kills a thousand at one blow.	*People think that Nazar fought and killed a thousand people at one time.*
Nazar shouts in the forest because he is afraid.	The man with the horse thinks that
Nazar sees the giants and crawls under the banner.	The giants think that
Nazar is riding on the back of the tiger.	The people think that
Nazar rides toward the enemy, carrying a large part of a tree.	The enemy thinks that

Exploring the Meaning

A. Getting the Deeper Meaning

Discuss these questions about the story.

1. What does this story say about people's opinions of others?
2. What does this story say about leaders?
3. Why is this story so funny?
4. What is this story's definition of a hero?

B. *Writing a Newspaper Article*

Imagine that you are a newspaper reporter who is writing a story about the mighty Nazar. In the article, tell:

- how Nazar helped the villagers kill a frightening tiger
- how he fought the enemy
- what people in the country think about him

Give the article a short, interesting title. Share your article with the class.

C. *In Everyday Life*

Discuss these questions.

1. Which do you like better, funny stories or serious ones? Why?
2. What makes a person a true hero?

The Shah Weaves a Rug

Iranian

Ancient Persia, in the western part of Asia, was the center of a great civilization and a huge empire. The Persians also built palaces, many of which contained beautiful rugs. Until recent times, a "shah" ruled Persia, or Iran, which is its modern name. This is about a shah of the past who faces a real challenge and who finds a very clever solution. In this folktale, you will also discover why Persian rugs are still valued throughout the world.

Before You Read

Talk about these questions.

1. Have you ever seen a Persian rug or a copy of a Persian rug? What colors and kinds of patterns do these rugs have?
2. Why do you think real Persian carpets are so expensive?
3. Many people have hobbies that they do in their free time. Do you have any hobbies?

Understanding Key Words

Read the sentences. You will find the words in **bold** in the story. Discuss what each word means.

1. No one knew why people were disappearing every night. It was a **mystery** where they were going.
2. The **bandits** were evil people. They stole from other people.
3. The bandit chief was **greedy.** He always wanted more money.
4. The shah was very **skilled** at making rugs. He knew how to weave beautiful rugs.
5. The people who were caught went to their **doom.** They faced a terrible future.
6. The soldier **seized** the bandit and tied him up. They grabbed him and held him.

Words about the Time and Place

You will find these words in the story.

beggar	a person who asks people for money in a public place
bewitched	under the power of a magic spell
caravan	a group of people traveling together through a dangerous place to somewhere safer
courtyard	an open space in the middle of a building
fort	a strong building made to keep enemies out
loom	a simple machine for weaving threads into cloth
spell	magic words that make something happen
weave	to make a cloth by pulling threads together (past forms: *wove, woven)*

The Shah Weaves a Rug

The king of Persia was called a shah. Some shahs were good, and others were not so good. The shah in this story was the best ruler Persia had ever had. Good people of that land who obeyed its laws loved him, but the bad people who did not obey the laws of their land were afraid of this shah. This shah was clever, and his heart was big. Often he would hide by wearing the rags of a beggar. No one knew who he was when he slipped out of his palace to walk on the city streets and along the country roads. In this way, he could see for himself what was going on in the land.

There was a time when bad news was spread throughout the shah's city. Everyone whispered, "People are disappearing each night. No one knows what becomes of them." The word was brought to the ears of the shah. Day after day, the same report was made. Wives came to the palace seeking their husbands and husbands came whose wives could not be found.

"I must look into this mystery for myself," the shah decided. He put on the clothes of a farmer and went into the marketplace.

People were selling and buying. Above the noise of many voices was heard the sound of sweet singing. The clear tones of the song rang out like the bells of a temple.

Under the shade of a tree, men and women had gathered around a singer dressed as a holy man.

"What can this be?" The shah stopped to listen at the edge of the crowd. "Who is this holy man that has never been brought to sing for me in the palace?"

The singer began to move backward. Under the shade tree, he backed little by little into a street that led out of the city. But he kept on singing. It seemed that his listeners were under a spell, for they moved after him. He slowly led them on. Farther and farther they followed him until the houses of the city were left behind them.

"This is strange!" The shah could not explain what was happening. So he went along to find out what it all meant.

At last, the singer came to the courtyard of an ancient fort that was no longer used. And as if by magic, the great gates of the fort were opened wide. Still singing loud and clear, the holy man walked backward in through the gates with the listeners following him.

"These people are being held in a magic spell!" the shah said to himself. "I must follow this to the end." So he, too, followed the singer in through the iron gates.

"Clang!" The great gates swung shut. Then a huge iron bar dropped across them. It was too late.

The song died. A crowd of strong men with fast-swinging clubs

rushed out and began to attack the frightened listeners. Soon every man and woman was tied hand and foot, including the shah.

"What will you do with us?" the shah asked those who were dragging him into the fort.

"Sell you in the slave market in a neighboring land," he was told. "You are strong and well fed. You will bring a good price. As soon as the moon shows its face over the desert, our caravan will leave."

"So this answers the mystery of why so many have disappeared." It was all clear to the shah now. Then he spoke to the captors.

"But I will not bring you nearly as much money in the slave market as I could right here. There is a way I am worth very much more. Let me speak to your chief."

Well, the leader of the bandits was always greedy for more money. "Let him tell us about this money he promises," the leader shouted to the men who had tied the shah up.

"I am a skilled weaver, although I am dressed like a farmer," said the shah. The words were true. When the shah was only a boy, he had learned from the palace weavers how to make a carpet. He loved the bright colors of the silk and wool threads. No one could weave a more beautiful rug than he.

"My fingers make magic on the weaving looms. The rug I can make for you will be worth three times my price as a slave."

"Go bring a loom." The leader's greedy eyes were shining. "Let this weaver show us his magic. If he has lied, we can sell him in the slave market on our next trip."

Each day the bandits watched the shah working at the loom. The chief of the bandits was very pleased when he saw the bright colors woven into beautiful flowers and birds.

"How much should I ask for this rug?" he asked the shah who was nearly finished.

"Five thousand gold coins."

"Five thousand! Who would pay so much?"

"The shah himself would pay it, but I am told he is away from the city just now. Take it to his queen. She also loves beautiful rugs. No doubt she will pay you that much."

"You speak intelligently," the head bandit said. "I will take the rug to the queen when you have finished."

The shah's fingers flew faster. He seemed to take special care with the pattern on the rug's end. The flowers and birds matched those in the rug's center. But there were also letters like those in old Persian writings. The bandits had never seen letters like these before. Such writing was known only to people of royal families. At last, the shah's rug was finished.

"I myself will go with the porter to carry the rug to the palace," the chief bandit said. "I will give it to the queen. If you are right, Weaver, I will come back here with five thousand gold coins."

"Unroll the rug only under the eyes of the queen herself," the shah said. "Do not let the gatekeeper or the doorkeeper stop you."

"The shah is not here. The queen is broken-hearted. She will see no one." At first, the guards would not let the bandit and his porter into the courtyard.

"But I have a rich gift for the queen." The bandit would not go away. "She will be angry if you do not let us come in."

So the gatekeeper let them pass. They entered the queen's part of the palace. There a guard also stopped them.

"I will take your gift to the queen. And I will let you know if it pleases her." The doorkeeper was going to turn the strangers way when the voice of the queen came from behind her curtains.

"Let the strangers come in," she cried out. "I will look at his gift. It will take away from my heart the worry I feel because of my husband's absence."

So the curtains were put aside and the chief bandit bowed low for the queen. Her dark eyes looked curiously over the veil that hid the lower part of her face.

When the rug was spread out, a cry of joy came from her lips. This was a rug of great beauty, like those already in the palace.

Then the queen gave another cry—a cry of surprise. She bent down to examine the end of the rug. She read it like a book. Then she said, "This is a rich gift, O Stranger. I accept it with pleasure. How much is it?"

"Five thousand gold coins for you, my Queen." The bandit bowed very low. "For someone else it would be more than twice that amount."

"Ten thousand gold coins. I shall give you that sum because the rug pleases me very much." Calling one of her guards, she added, "I myself will go with this man to count the coins. You, Stranger, wait here until we return."

In this way, the queen had a chance to give secret orders to the palace guards.

"Into the pattern of that rug," she told them, "our shah has woven a message for me. He calls for help. This man who has brought me the rug holds him prisoner in an old fort outside the city walls. When these men leave, follow them. Give orders to fifty of our best warriors to follow you. Be sure that the gates of the fort do not close before you rescue the shah."

The chief bandit knew nothing of the message that the shah had woven into the border of the rug. Because he was so happy about the bags of gold, the bandit did not see the shah's soldiers following him.

When the chief bandit and the porter came back to the fort, they met the false holy man, who was singing. Another group of bewitched listeners was following him.

The chief bandit stopped to let them pass inside the iron gates. His cruel eyes shone with satisfaction as he watched the last one go to his doom.

But before he could enter the courtyard, the fifty strong palace soldiers had fallen on him. Before the gate could swing shut, they had captured the bandits. The soldier seized the false holy man with the sweet singing voice, and they tied up the bandit chief.

With their shining swords, the shah's men quickly took over the fort. They freed their shah and the people who had just fallen under the spell of the singer.

These men and women fell to their knees before the good shah, who had saved them from the slave market. With all the people of the city, they celebrated after the chief and his band were put to death.

"Blessed be weavers!" This saying was heard all over Persia. And from that day to this, this country has been famous for its beautiful rugs.

Understanding the Story

A. What Happens?

Match the sentence parts. Write the correct letter in each blank.

____ 1.	The news spreads through the city	a. the people are controlled by a magic spell.
____ 2.	The shah dresses	b. catch the false holy man and the bandit chief.
____ 3.	As the false holy man sings,	c. through the gates of the fort, everyone is locked inside.
____ 4.	After the holy man walks	d. that people are disappearing.
____ 5.	A gang of bandits	e. understands the message the shah wrote for her.
____ 6.	The bandit chief	f. sell the people who followed the holy man in a slave market.
____ 7.	The queen	g. like a farmer and walks through the streets.
____ 8.	The shah's soldiers	h. is greedy and agrees to let the shah weave a rug.

B. Looking Back

Answer these questions about the story.

1. How does the shah find out what is really going on in his country?
2. What mystery does the shah decide to solve?
3. What strange happening does the shah see and hear?
4. How does the shah convince the bandits not to sell him at the slave market?
5. How does the queen save the shah?
6. What happens to the bandits?

C. Understanding Characters' Reasons

Complete the chart to explain the characters' actions.

Questions	Explanations
Why does the shah walk through the streets dressed so that no one will know him?	*He wants to know what is going on in the land. He wants to look into the mystery.*
Why does the shah dress like a farmer and go to the marketplace?	
Why do the people follow the singer?	
Why does the shah weave a rug?	
Why does the queen give a cry of surprise when she sees the rug?	
Why does the queen go off to count the money?	
Why do the soldiers follow the bandit?	

Exploring the Meaning

A. Getting the Deeper Meaning

Answer these questions.

1. Compare what happens to the plans of the "enemy" in this story to what happens to the plans of the enemy in "The Lucky Charm." What do both these folktales tell about the lives of criminals?

2. Why is the shah a good ruler?

B. Telling the Story Again

Do these activities.

1. Imagine that you are the queen. Tell the story from her point of view. In your story, you can tell:
   - how you felt when the shah was missing
   - what you thought happened to the shah
   - how you felt when you saw the shah's message
   - what happened after the end of the story

2. Imagine that you are one of the people who is following the holy man at the end of the story. In your story, you can tell:
   - how you felt when you heard the holy man's singing
   - what happened when you arrived at the fort
   - what happened to the bandits
   - what you think about the shah

C. In Everyday Life

Discuss these questions.

1. Have you ever heard the expression "Crime does not pay"? What does this mean? Why do so many stories present this as a main idea?

2. What makes a good leader or ruler?

3. The shah is a ruler, but he also knows how to make a rug. Why, do you think, is it important to have more than one skill?

PART THREE

Love and Marriage

The Tiger's Whisker

Korean

The tiger has always been very important in the life of the Korean people. If you look at a map of Korea, in the southeastern part of Asia, you will see that it looks like the body of a tiger. When the Olympics were held in Korea in 1988, the tiger was the symbol. In fact, a folk legend of Korea says that the country grew out of the marriage of a man and a tiger. When Korean children disobey their parents, they are often told, "If you don't behave better, the tiger will get you!" So it is not surprising that the tiger has an important part in this story from Korea. This folktale is about a very serious problem that a wife faces.

Before You Read

Discuss these questions.

1. What do you know about tigers?
2. What stories do you know about tigers and other wild animals?
3. When people have personal problems, who can they turn to for advice?

Understanding Key Words

Read the sentences. You will find the words in **bold** in the story. Discuss what each word means.

1. The woman is **depressed** because her husband does not seem to love her anymore.

2. The woman's husband speaks **roughly** to her. He shouts at her and shows no respect for her.

3. She needs a **whisker** from a tiger. She has to get one of the hairs that grow on the sides of the mouth of a fierce tiger!

4. She needs the whisker to make the magic drink. The whisker is an important **ingredient.**

5. The tiger's home is in a **cave.** It lives in an opening in the side of a mountain.

6. It is not easy to **tame** a tiger. The tiger is a wild animal that does not easily become friends with people.

7. A tiger is a very **vicious** animal. It will attack and kill a person.

8. She is very **patient** with the wild animal. She slowly becomes friends with it.

9. Yun Ok is **shocked** by the hermit's action. She is surprised and upset by what he has done.

Words about the Time and Place

You will find these words in the story.

hermit   a person who goes away from other people to live alone. A hermit is often a holy person.

potion   a powerful drink. In folktales, people who drink a magic potion are changed in some way.

rice   a grass whose seed is used for food. It is an important food in the countries of southeast Asia.

The Tiger's Whisker

One day a young woman named Yun Ok came to the house of a mountain hermit to get help. The hermit was a famous wise man who made lucky charms and magic potions.

When Yun Ok entered his house, the man asked, "Why are you here?"

Yun Ok said, "O Famous Wise Man, I am very depressed and worried. Make me a potion!"

"Yes, yes, make a potion! Everyone needs potions. We all think we can solve all our problems with a potion."

"Master," Yun Ok replied, "if you do not help me, I am truly lost!"

"Well, what is your story?" the man said, because he decided to listen.

"It is my husband," Yun Ok said. "He is very dear to me. For the past three years, he has been away fighting in the wars. Now that he has returned, he hardly speaks to me, or to anyone else. If I speak, he doesn't seem to hear. When he talks at all, it is roughly. If I serve him food that he doesn't like, he pushes it away and angrily leaves the room. Sometimes when he should be working in the rice field, I see him sitting on top of the hill, looking toward the sea."

"Yes, that sometimes happens when young men come back from the wars," the hermit said. "Go on."

"There is no more to tell, Learned One. I want a potion to give my husband so that he will be loving and gentle, as he used to be."

"Come back in three days and I will tell you what we shall need for a potion," said the hermit.

Three days later Yun Ok returned to the wise man's house. The wise man told her that the most important ingredient he needed in the potion was the whisker of a living tiger.

Yun Ok asked, "How could I possibly get the whisker of a living tiger?"

"If the potion is important enough, you will succeed," the hermit said.

Yun Ok went home. She thought about how she would get the tiger's whisker. Then one night when her husband was asleep, she crept from her house with a bowl of rice and meat sauce in her hand. She went to the place on the mountainside where the tiger lived. Standing far from the tiger's cave, she held out the bowl of food, calling the tiger to come and eat. The tiger did not come.

The next night Yun Ok went again, this time a little bit closer. Again she offered a bowl of rice to the tiger. Every night Yun Ok went to the mountain, each time a few steps nearer to the tiger's cave than she had been the night before. Little by little the tiger became used to seeing her there.

One night Yun Ok came very close to the tiger's cave. This time the tiger came a few steps toward her and stopped. The two of them stood looking at one another in the moonlight. It happened again the following night, and this time they were so close that Yun Ok could talk to the tiger in a soft voice. The next night, after looking carefully into Yun Ok's eyes, the tiger ate the food that she held out for him. After that when Yun Ok came in the night, she found the tiger waiting for her. After the tiger ate, Yun Ok gently rubbed his head with her hand. Nearly six months had passed since the night of her first visit. One night, after patting the animal, Yun Ok said:

"O Tiger, I must have one of your whiskers. Do not be angry!"

And she cut off one of the whiskers.

As Yun Ok had expected, the tiger did not become angry. She went down the trail, not walking but running, with the whisker in her hand.

The next morning she was at the mountain hermit's house at dawn. "O Famous One!" she shouted, "I have the tiger's whisker! Now you can make the potion you promised, so my husband will be loving and gentle again!"

The hermit took the whisker and examined it. Satisfied that it had really come from a tiger, he leaned forward and dropped it into the fire that was burning in his fireplace.

"Oh, what have you done with it?" the woman called out, shocked by the hermit's action.

"Tell me how you got it," the hermit said.

"I went to the mountain each night with a little bowl of food. At first, I stood far away, and I came a little closer each time, to win the tiger's confidence. I spoke gently and kindly to him, to make him understand I wanted to please him. I was patient. Each night I brought him food although I knew that he would not eat. But I did not give up. I came again and again. I never spoke loudly. I never said anything mean to him. Then one night he took a few steps toward me. After that, he began to meet me on the trail and eat out of the bowl that I held in my hands. I rubbed his head, and he made happy sounds in his throat. Only then did I take the whisker."

"Yes," the hermit said, "you tamed the tiger and won his confidence and love."

"But you have thrown the whisker into the fire!" Yun Ok said. "I did all that for nothing!"

"No, I do not think it is all for nothing," the hermit said. "The whisker is no longer needed. Yun Ok, let me ask you, is a man more vicious than a tiger? Does he respond less to kindness and understanding? If you can win the love and confidence of a wild and bloodthirsty animal by kindness and patience, surely you can do the same with your husband."

Hearing this, Yun Ok stood for a moment without saying a word. Then she went down the trail, thinking about the truth she had learned in the house of the hermit.

Understanding the Story

A. What Happens?

Match the sentence parts. Write the correct letter in each blank.

_____ 1. Yun Ok says that her husband

a. closer to the tiger's cave.

_____ 2. Yun Ok asks

b. is no more difficult to handle than the tiger.

_____ 3. The hermit says that we think we

c. the whisker from the tiger.

_____ 4. The hermit tells her

d. when the hermit throws the whisker into the fire.

_____ 5. Each night Yun Ok comes

e. can solve our problems with a potion.

_____ 6. Yun Ok cuts

f. shows her no respect or kindness.

_____ 7. Yun Ok is surprised

g. to get the whisker from a tiger for a potion.

_____ 8. The hermit says that her husband

h. the hermit to help her.

B. Looking Back

Discuss these questions about the story.

1. Why does Yun Ok visit the hermit?
2. What does she want the hermit to give her?
3. How does Yun Ok finally get one of the tiger's whiskers?
4. Why does the hermit throw the whisker into the fire?
5. What lesson about life does Yun Ok learn from the hermit?

C. *Understanding the Parts of the Story*

Complete the chart to show the main parts of the story.

The characters in the story (People/animals):	
Where the story takes place:	
Problems: 1. Yun Ok's problem at the beginning of the story: 2. Yun Ok's problem after the hermit agrees to make the potion:	1. 2.
What do you think Yun Ok will do after the story ends?	

Exploring the Meaning

A. *Getting the Deeper Meaning*

Discuss these questions about the story.

1. What does this folktale tell us makes a happy marriage?
2. Why, do you think, does the husband act the way he does?
3. The hermit says that everyone wants potions. Why, do you think, do so many people want potions? What is the problem with using potions?

B. *Writing Letters to Get and Give Advice*

1. Imagine that you are Yun Ok and you decide to write a letter to get advice. You are writing to the author of a newspaper column who helps people with their personal problems. In your letter:

   - tell how your husband is acting
   - tell why this is a problem for you
   - ask for help with your problem

2. Now imagine that you are the author of the newspaper column. Write a letter giving advice to Yun Ok. You can use the advice given by the hermit in the story or think of ideas of your own.

3. Share your letters with the group. What different advice is given? What is the best advice?

C. *In Everyday Life*

Discuss these questions.

1. What are some of the reasons for divorces in the modern world?

2. Why do some countries still have very few divorces?

3. What can a husband and wife do to keep a marriage together?

The Giant's Bride

Scandinavian

Scandinavia is a region in the northern part of Europe. It includes the countries of Norway, Sweden, and Denmark. The winters are very cold and long. Among the groups of people who live in Scandinavia are the Lapps. The reindeer is very important in the lives of the Lapps. They use the reindeer for food and to pull their sleighs over the snow. The Lapps do not stay in one place. Instead, they travel from place to place so their reindeer can find enough food to eat. You will learn more about the lives of the Lapps in this story.

Before You Read

Discuss these questions.

1. What do you know about reindeer? Do you know any songs about them?

2. There are many wedding customs. For example, in some cultures, the bride's family gives money to the groom's family. In other cultures, the groom gives money to the bride's family. What wedding customs do you know about?

Understanding Key Words

Read the sentences. You will find the words in **bold** in the story. Discuss what each word means.

1. The Lapps **wander** around the countryside. They do not stay in one place.

2. The giants get angry and shout at one another very often. They **quarrel** with each other all the time.

3. The Lapp and his daughter do not want to say no to the giant's request. They are afraid that the giant will **lose his temper.** They know that giants get angry very easily.

4. The Lapp and his daughter **put off** marriage. They say the marriage will take place some time in the future.

5. The giant keeps thinking that his bride is **shy** and **bashful.** She is quiet and does not say anything when he talks to her.

6. The giant tries to catch the Lapp and his daughter, but it is all **in vain.** He is not able to find them.

7. He cannot **bear** the laughter of the other giants, so he runs away.

Words about the Time and Place

You will find these words in the story.

cliff	a side of a mountain that goes straight up and down, like a wall
dowry	money or property a woman or her father brings to her husband as a gift before the wedding
harness	to tie a large animal to a wagon so it can be used to pull the wagon
herd	a group of animals that live and travel together
log	a thick, round piece of wood
moss	very small green plants that grow on the ground or on trees
sledge	a kind of big sled, used to pull people across ice or snow
stool	a small chair with no arms or back
veil	a thin piece of cloth, sometimes used to cover a woman's face

---

The Giant's Bride

There were many giants in the northern parts of Norway, Finland, and Sweden. And there were also the Lapps, who were tiny compared to the giants. Both the giants and the Lapps used to wander around the countryside, following the reindeer herds.

The giants were grumpy people, always quarreling with each other. When they quarreled, they yelled and threw great lumps of ice or rocks. The little Lapp people were afraid of them. Because the giants made so much noise, the Lapps' reindeer herds sometimes panicked, rushed away for miles, or even fell over cliffs and drowned.

The Lapps tried to keep out of the way of the giants, but it wasn't always possible. Lapps have to wander from place to place to find food for their herds. They also have to set up their tents, light their fires, and feed their reindeer.

One day a rich Lapp was driving in his sledge with his daughter. They came to a place that had moss for their reindeer to eat, so they set up their tent. They didn't know that a giant lived nearby.

This wasn't a bad giant. He fell in love with the Lapp girl and wanted to marry her. Neither the girl nor her father was pleased about that.

When the giant said that he would like to marry the girl, they did not say no because they were afraid he would lose his temper. They pretended to be honored and pleased.

But they kept putting the marriage off. The girl was miserable about having that stupid giant for a husband, and her father didn't want him for a son-in-law. He was a good father and didn't want to force the girl into something she didn't want to do.

Meanwhile the giant would sit near their tent, with a smile all over his huge, silly face, and call the girl "my little darling."

The poor Lapps wondered what they should do. The giant was lazy and stupid, but giants did have awful tempers. If any one of them was angry, he might want to eat a girl instead of marrying her! Whatever happened, the Lapps decided, they must keep the giant happy.

At that time, this is what would happen at a wedding of the Lapps: A bridegroom would come to the bride's tent on the wedding day. Then the bride's father would come out and go with the bridegroom to the reindeer. Together they would decide which of the reindeer were to be the bride's dowry. While they were out, the bride would get dressed in her very best woolen dress, put on a red cap, a silver belt, a new pair of shoes, and a thick veil. When the father and the bridegroom returned, the father would say the marriage words over them, and go away, leaving the bride and the bridegroom together.

The two little Lapps thought they could trick the giant. The father looked around and found a log about the same size as his daughter. He carved it, forming a head and arms. His daughter put her best clothes on the log: a woolen dress, a new red cap, and a silver belt. She set a nice pair of shoes in front of it. Then they put it on a stool at the dark end of the tent. They covered its top with a veil. They were satisfied by what they saw.

The girl got out the sledge. She loaded it with their spare tent and everything else she thought could be taken without making the tent look too bare and empty. Then she harnessed their reindeer to the sledge and drove off to a hidden place on the other side of the hill. Meanwhile, her father waited for the giant.

The girl hadn't been gone long when the giant arrived. Her father welcomed him into the tent. When the giant looked around, he saw the veiled figure. He greeted his bride, but of course, there was no answer.

"Shy and bashful!" said her father, shaking his head.

"The little darling!" said the giant fondly.

"I'm sure she'll make you a good wife even if she is a bit shy at first," said the father.

After this, they went out to count the reindeer for the daughter's dowry. They argued for a while. Then they agreed, and the Lapp showed the giant a reindeer he had already killed for the marriage supper. Then the father quickly said the marriage words over the bridegroom and the veiled figure. After this, the father said goodbye. Without going back into the tent, he hurried off as fast as he could to where his daughter was waiting in the sledge.

The giant went into the tent, where a bright fire was burning.

"Now, my little darling," he said to his bride, "the meat is already in the pot. Put the pot on the fire!"

Of course, there was no answer.

"Oh, the little dear is so bashful," went on the giant, "I'll have to do it myself!"

After a while, the pot began to boil and then it boiled over.

"Move the pot aside a little, my darling girl!" said the giant.

Still no answer.

"My little one is bashful!" he said again. "I must do it myself."

When the meat was cooked, he tried again.

"Come, now, my dear, please serve."

But the bride was as shy as before and did not move.

"Oh, how bashful she is. I must do it myself," repeated the giant.

When he had put the meat on the dishes, he invited her to come and eat, but nothing happened. The bride did not move.

"I will have more," thought the giant and he began to eat with a good appetite. When he had eaten the reindeer meat, he asked his bride to get the bed ready.

"My love, are you so bashful? Must I do it myself?" said the simple giant.

But now at last when there was still no answer, he lost his patience and grabbed the log that was dressed as his bride. He shook it. Only then did he find out how he had been tricked. He had gotten a block of wood instead of a girl. Naturally he was enraged and started to chase the two Lapps.

But all was in vain, for they had too great a start. Even the giant could not find them. It was snowing, and the falling snow hid their tracks.

Searching for them, the giant lost his way in the mountains and felt very cold. When the moon came up, he was shivering so hard that all he could think about was the blazing fire in the Lapps' tent. Anybody but a giant would have frozen to death before reaching the tent, but the giant did not. He was sick and sore the next morning, but not dead.

When the other giants heard about what happened, they laughed at him so much that he couldn't bear it. He went off by himself and was never seen again.

Understanding the Story

A. When Does It Happen?

Show the order in which the events in the story happen. Write the correct number in the blank.

____ The father carves a head and arms on the log to make it look like his daughter.

____ The girl loads up her sledge and rides off.

____ The other giants laugh at him when they hear the story.

_1_ The giant tells the Lapp and his daughter he wants to marry her.

____ The girl dresses the log in her best clothes.

____ The Lapp and his daughter pretend to be happy that the giant wants to marry her.

____ The enraged giant tries to find the Lapp and his daughter.

____ The Lapp and the giant count the reindeer for the bride's dowry.

B. Looking Back

Discuss these questions about the story.

1. Why are the Lapps afraid of the giants?
2. Why doesn't the Lapp girl want to marry the giant?
3. How do the Lapp girl and her father trick the giant?
4. Why does the giant think that his bride isn't speaking to him?
5. Why does the giant become so angry?

C. Understanding the Details

Complete the chart. Look back at the story to find information about the Lapps.

What Lapp homes are like:	The Lapps live in tents.
The furniture in their homes:	
What Lapps eat:	
Why Lapps move from place to place:	
What the father of the bride has to do before a Lapp wedding:	
What the wedding ceremony is like:	

Exploring the Meaning

A. *Getting the Deeper Meaning*

Discuss these questions about the story.

1. What makes this story so funny?

2. Compare the humor in this story to the humor in "Nazar the Brave" (see pages 65–69). How are the main characters in these two stories alike? How are they different?

3. The Lapp and his daughter play their trick on the giant because they believe giants can be easily fooled. What stories do you know about people being tricked because they are silly or foolish?

4. Do you feel glad or sorry for the giant when he is tricked? Explain.

B. *Solving the Problem*

Discuss the following.

The Lapp does not want his daughter to marry the giant. The daughter does not want to marry the giant. Together they think of a way to trick the giant. Can you think of another solution to the problem? Work in a small group and write down as many solutions as you can. Share your ideas with the class.

C. *In Everyday Life*

Discuss these questions.

1. Why do parents sometimes get upset if someone from another culture wants to marry their son or daughter?

2. What advantages or disadvantages are there in marrying a person from another culture?

The Love Crystal

Vietnamese

A common theme in stories and songs is how unreturned love often breaks people's hearts. Such a theme is explored in this story from Vietnam, a country in southeast Asia. In this story, you will read about a beautiful young woman kept locked in a tower and the song of a fisherman. As you read, try to guess what will happen to the young woman.

Crystals are colorless stones that look like glass. They are sometimes carved to make beautiful objects. You will find out why the crystal in this story is so special.

Before You Read

Discuss these questions.

1. There are many stories about people who are sad because their love is not returned by the person they love. Do you know of any?

2. Many people like happy stories better than sad stories. But what can people learn from sad stories?

Understanding Key Words

Read the sentences. You will find the words in **bold** in the story. Discuss what each word means.

1. The young woman believes that **Fate** will choose the man she is going to marry. She thinks that a powerful force that rules the world will choose her husband.

2. The young woman is waiting for the man who is **destined** to be her husband. She believes that Fate will bring her a husband.

3. The fisherman plays a **melancholy** song, but the sad music fills the young woman with joy.

4. It is **forbidden** to look at the mandarin's daughter. Strangers are not permitted to see her.

5. The young woman has no hope that he will return. She **despairs** of ever seeing him again.

6. The woman looks away **in disgust** from the fisherman's ugly face. It sickens her to see such ugliness.

7. She is very sad when she sees the picture of the fisherman in the cup. She feels **sorrow** for what she has done.

8. There is a **magnificent** crystal next to the fisherman's body. It is an unusually beautiful one.

Words About the Time and Place

You will find these words in the story.

embroider	to sew pretty designs on cloth
flute	a small musical instrument that is round and narrow. You blow into it to make music.
maid	a woman servant who usually works inside the house
mandarin	a high official in the Chinese empire
tower	the narrow top part of a building. It rises above the lower parts.

The Love Crystal

Long ago a beautiful young girl lived in a palace in a peaceful land near a calm river. Her father was a great mandarin. She was so beautiful that no one was allowed to look at her except the members of the palace. In order to keep his daughter out of the sight of strangers, the mandarin had her kept in a tower that stood above the river. She passed many lonely hours there embroidering and reading, waiting for the man who was destined to make her his bride.

She often looked out upon the river below and dreamt of all the places the river had been. One day as she looked out at the river, she saw a poor fisherman sailing his small boat. She could not see him well from such a height, but from the distance he looked young and strong. He played a flute. Its melody rose sweet and clear to the tower from which the mandarin's daughter looked down at him. The sad music of the flute filled her with joy and wonder. As she listened, she was deeply moved by the gentle, melancholy melody. It told her about faraway places she would never see. It spoke to her about feelings for which there are no words and about everything beautiful on earth.

Day after day, the fisherman played his flute as his small boat passed the tower in which the lonely girl listened, carried away with love and joy. She thought that he was really some prince whom Fate planned for her to marry. As she listened, she threw down flower petals to show him how delighted she was with his music.

The fisherman knew that a young girl lived in the tower. When the flower petals drifted down to him, he knew that she liked his songs. He thought that she must be beautiful, even though he had never seen her face clearly.

And so a connection grew between them that was made of his songs and her pleasure in hearing them. As she listened to his flute and he caught the softly falling petals, they both thought only the best thoughts about each other.

One day the fisherman did not appear. He had learned that the girl in the tower was the mandarin's daughter. Because it was forbidden for a stranger to see her, he did not dare return. The mandarin's daughter waited and waited for him, but the river remained empty. Despairing that he would ever return, she refused to leave the window or to eat or sleep. She watched the moon all night, praying that the fisherman and his flute would return. As the days passed and the fisherman never came, she became pale and thin. Her tears turned to silence.

Doctors tried to discover what caused her to wilt and fade like a flower, but they failed. The mandarin and his wife didn't know what to do to save their daughter's life. Finally their daughter's maid told the mandarin about the fisherman and his charming songs.

The mandarin had the fisherman brought to the palace. The poor fisherman was young and strong as the young girl had imagined, but his face was ugly.

"Although you are only a fisherman," said the mandarin, "your songs are the key to my daughter's health. Perhaps Fate has destined you to become her husband. Let's see if she will love you as much as she loves your music."

The fisherman was deeply moved by what he heard. "I did not want to have the power of life and death over your daughter," he said. "I only played my songs for her because she liked them. I have never even seen her face."

The fisherman was taken to the foot of the tower and told to play the flute. When the young woman heard the music, she was delighted. She rushed down from the tower to the fisherman. When she discovered how ugly he was, she was unable to speak and turned away in disgust. She could not even bring herself to thank him for the music.

When the fisherman saw the mandarin's daughter, he fell in love with her. But when she turned away from him, he realized that his love was hopeless. Sadly he went away and sadly the mandarin's daughter returned to the tower. Although she was no longer sick, something beautiful had gone out of her life.

The fisherman never again returned to his boat and the young woman never again heard his flute. In time, she almost forgot him, except for the echo of his music in her dreams. She continued to live in the tower, waiting for the prince who never came.

But not long after, the fisherman died because he realized that the mandarin's daughter could not return his love. All his beauty was in his music and not in his face, and the young woman wanted only his songs.

Before he was buried, his family found a magnificent crystal next to his body. Everyone realized that the crystal was made of his unanswered love. The family put it into the front of his boat as a remembrance, and they threw the flute into the river.

One day as the mandarin was in a boat on the river, he saw the fisherman's boat with the shining crystal in it. When he heard why it was there, he was strongly moved and bought it. Then one of the glassblowers made it into a magnificent teacup.

The cup was strange and wonderful. When tea was poured into it, the picture of the fisherman appeared in it. As the tea moved around in the cup, one could faintly hear the music of the flute.

Because he thought that it would please his daughter, the mandarin took the crystal cup to her. But when she saw the fisherman's image and heard the flute song, she was filled with sorrow. But she asked to be left alone with the cup.

When everyone left, she poured tea into the cup and held it in her hands. As she looked into it, she saw and heard the fisherman as clearly as if he were again on the river. Then she realized that a heart that can make music is more important than an ugly face. Our faces are given to us, but we can control our hearts. She understood that the fisherman had loved her enough to die, and her failure to return his love had caused his death.

As the young woman cried quietly, her tears fell into the cup. The crystal disappeared because her tears were made of love, which brought peace at last to the fisherman's soul.

Later, they found the girl sitting beside the window. Her body no longer had a soul. She was as still as stone. They heard the faint sound of flute music from the river. They all knew that the mandarin's beautiful daughter and the fisherman were at last together in happiness.

Understanding the Story

A. *What Happens?*

Complete each sentence by choosing **a, b,** or **c.** Circle the letter of what you think is the correct answer.

1. Why does the mandarin keep his daughter locked up?
   a. He wants to keep people from seeing her.
   b. He wants to punish her for falling in love.
   c. He wants to show he controls her.

2. Why does a connection grow between the fisherman and the mandarin's daughter?
   a. She falls in love with him because he is handsome.
   b. He falls in love with her because she is the mandarin's daughter.
   c. She loves to listen to his beautiful songs.

3. How does the mandarin's daughter let the fisherman know that she is listening to his songs?
   a. She tells him.
   b. She throws flower petals down to him.
   c. She throws feathers down to him.

4. Why does the fisherman disappear one day?
   a. He finds out she is the mandarin's daughter.
   b. He gets tired of playing for the girl in the tower.
   c. The mandarin tells him he must leave or die.

5. What happens to the fisherman?
   a. He marries the mandarin's daughter.
   b. He marries a different girl.
   c. He dies of a broken heart.

6. What happens to the young girl?
   a. She dies of a broken heart.
   b. She marries the fisherman.
   c. She marries someone else.

B. Looking Back

Discuss these questions about the story.

1. Why are the fisherman's songs important to the mandarin's daughter?
2. What happens to the mandarin's daughter after the fisherman disappears?
3. What mistake does she make when she looks at the fisherman standing next to her?
4. Why is this folktale called "The Love Crystal"?
5. What gives this sad love story a happy ending?

C. Understanding the Characters' Problems

Complete the chart on this page and page 108. Write the problems or the solutions.

Character	Problem	Solution
Mandarin	1. He doesn't want strangers to see his daughter.	1. He keeps her in a tower above the river.
	2.	2. The mandarin brings the fisherman to the palace.
The Mandarin's Daughter	1. The fisherman is too far away to talk to.	1.
	2.	2. She refuses to eat or sleep and stops crying.

	3. She learns the fisherman died because she thought he was ugly and would not return his love.	3.
The Fisherman	1. He learns that the young girl listening to his flute is the mandarin's daughter.	1.
	2. The mandarin's daughter does not want to look at him because he is ugly.	2.

Exploring the Meaning

A. Getting the Deeper Meaning

Discuss these questions about the story.

1. What are some reasons the daughter of the mandarin is so unhappy?
2. The mandarin's daughter realizes she acted foolishly, but it is too late because the fisherman is dead. How should she have treated the ugly fisherman?

3. We learn that the mandarin makes his daughter suffer without meaning to. What does the mandarin do later in the story that shows he really loves her?

4. What else can the fisherman do when the mandarin's daughter rejects him?

B. *Adding New Endings*

1. Give the story a different ending. Tell what would have happened if the mandarin's daughter had not turned away from the fisherman. Would this have been a better (or worse) ending than the one we have? Why?

2. Tell what would happen if the fisherman was still alive when the mandarin's daughter realizes her mistake. Why would this be a better (or worse) ending than the one in the story?

C. *In Everyday Life*

Discuss these questions.

1. Why do you think some parents try to stop their young adult children from dating other young people? What can the young person do?

2. What does the ugly fisherman who plays beautiful music tell us about people in real life?

3. What are some advantages of being good-looking or "beautiful"? What are the disadvantages? What do you think being "good-looking" or "beautiful" really means?

How Juan Married a Princess

Filipino

The Philippines are a group of islands in the Pacific Ocean, east of the Asian mainland. People came to these islands 5,000 years ago. Because Spain ruled the Philippines from the 1500s until the end of the 1800s, many Filipinos, as people who live on the islands are called, have Spanish names. In fact, the main character of "Why Juan Married a Princess" has a Spanish name. This story is not the typical "rags to riches" folktale. In "Cinderella," "Snow White," and many other folktales, a prince marries a beautiful girl who is poor. In this tale, a poor boy marries a princess.

Before You Read

Discuss these questions.

1. Try to guess how it happens that a poor boy can marry a princess.
2. The "happy ending" of many folktales has a poor girl marry a prince. Why do many people think this is a happy ending?
3. In folktales, fathers "give" their daughters in marriage. Where in the world is this still true? Why is this no longer true in many countries?

Understanding Key Words

Read the sentences. You will find the words in **bold** in the story. Discuss what each word means.

1. Juan likes to **gamble.** But when he plays games for money, he usually loses.
2. Juan sets out to **seek his fortune.** He has no money, so he decides to look for a better life in a different place.
3. The cake is Juan's **property.** He bought it and it belongs to him.
4. Juan explains his reasons for taking things. The people who hear Juan are **confused.** They don't really understand what Juan means.
5. Juan **takes a nap** in front of a shop. He doesn't plan to sleep long.
6. Juan sits down on a **riverbank** to rest. The side of the river is a pleasant place.
7. **By chance,** Juan sees the princess come to the river. He does not plan to see her.
8. Juan speaks **boldly** to the princess. Juan is not afraid to go up to the princess and talk to her.
9. Juan's **argument** is difficult to understand. He gives reasons, but people do not understand them.
10. The king does not **protest** Juan's demand. He agrees to Juan's request right away.

Words about the Time and Place

You will find these words in the story.

barbershop a place where a man goes to get a shave and a haircut

centavo a small coin. One hundred centavos equal one peso. The peso is the basic unit of money in the Philippines.

How Juan Married a Princess

Once there was a man named Juan who spent all his time gambling. Sometimes he was lucky and won a little money, but usually he lost.

One day after losing every cent he had, Juan decided to leave the city, where bad luck seemed to follow him. Without a penny to his name, he set out to seek his fortune bravely and cheerfully.

Suddenly Juan saw something shining in the dust. When he bent down to see what it was, he found a centavo.

"Now I can gamble my luck with this one centavo and see what it will bring me!" he said to himself.

Juan took the centavo to the nearest village and spent it on a small cake. Although he was hungry, Juan ate only a part of the cake. He wrapped the rest and put it carefully into his pocket. Then he continued to walk around in the village. Soon he became sleepy and sat down outside a small shop to rest.

As soon as Juan had fallen asleep, a chicken came by, saw the piece of cake sticking out of Juan's pocket, and began to eat it. This woke Juan up. He grabbed the chicken by the neck.

"What are you doing to my chicken?" shouted an angry voice. The owner of the chicken stood in the doorway of the shop.

"Your chicken has eaten my cake," said Juan. "The cake belonged to me, and the cake is now inside the chicken. I must take the chicken to take back my property, the cake. The chicken now belongs to me, doesn't it?"

The owner of the chicken was confused by Juan's thinking, so he agreed that Juan was right. Juan took the chicken.

Juan continued on his way and at last came to a second village. Here he again found a place to take a nap and was soon fast asleep. This time he was in front of a barbershop. The barbershop had a dog. While Juan was sleeping, the dog caught Juan's chicken and ate it up. When Juan woke up and realized that the dog had eaten the chicken, he grabbed the dog.

"What are you doing with my dog?" shouted the barber angrily.

"Your dog has eaten my chicken," said Juan. "Since my chicken is now in the dog's stomach, I must take the dog with me." He picked up the barber's dog and left the shop, with the barber staring confused after him.

As Juan continued on his way, he came to a tiny house. Juan was very thirsty from walking so far in the heat of the day. He decided to stop at this house to ask for some water. He tied his dog to the iron gate in front of the house and entered to ask for a drink of water. After he drank, he walked back to the gate to which he had tied the dog. While Juan was drinking, the gate had fallen on the poor animal and killed it. Juan pulled out one of the iron bars of the gate. "I have a right to take it," he said to himself.

"Why are you stealing one of my iron bars, you thief!" shouted the owner of the house at Juan.

"It killed my dog, so now it belongs to me!" shouted Juan as he walked off with the bar over his shoulder.

Juan continued on his way until he stopped by a river to rest. He sat down upon the riverbank. He entertained himself by tossing the iron bar up into the air and then catching it. But soon the bar fell into the water and was lost from sight.

"River," he said, "do you know that you now belong to me? Yes, my property is now inside of you. Therefore, you and what you contain is mine!"

Juan sat all day beside his river and watched to see if anyone would come to bathe in it.

By chance, this was the day for the princess to come to the river to have her bath. When Juan saw her coming near the river, he had an idea. He waited until her foot touched the water. Then he boldly came up to her and said, "O Princess, please listen to me. Know that since you are touching this water, you have placed your life in my hands!"

"How is that possible?" asked the princess curiously.

"This river in which you are bathing belongs to me. Since you have touched the water, you, too, are my property and I have the right to take you as mine!"

This announcement was so surprising to the princess that she didn't know what to say. Finally she said, "I do not know what to tell you, but if we ask my father, the king, he will surely know how to answer your demand."

Juan agreed that it would be fair to allow the king to hear his argument, so they went to tell the princess's father the whole story.

"I think, O King," Juan concluded, "that you can see very clearly how matters stand: the centavo was mine, the chicken ate the cake that the centavo paid for. The dog ate the chicken that had eaten the cake. The iron bar took the place of the dog it had killed. The river took the iron bar that killed the dog. The princess used the river that belonged to me because it took the bar that killed the dog that ate the chicken that ate the cake the centavo paid for. No one can question that the centavo was mine because I found it!"

The king could not argue with such brilliant thinking. Rather than try to protest, he agreed to let Juan marry his daughter. So Juan won the princess's hand and they lived happily ever after.

Understanding the Story

A. *What Happens?*

Complete each sentence by choosing **a, b,** or **c.** Circle the letter of the answer you think is correct.

1. Juan is a poor young man because
   - a. he has no father to help him.
   - b. he is too lazy to work.
   - c. he loses all his money by gambling.

2. He gets a chicken because
   - a. it eats part of his cake, so he says the chicken is his.
   - b. he works and earns the chicken as payment.
   - c. it is on his property, so he says it is his.

3. Juan gets the dog because
   - a. it follows him and the chicken.
   - b. it eats the chicken, so he says it is his property.
   - c. it bites him, so he says it is his.

4. Juan feels it is right to take an iron bar because
   - a. it falls on his leg and injures it.
   - b. it falls on his chicken and kills it.
   - c. it falls on his dog and kills it.

5. The king agrees to Juan's request because
   - a. Juan's argument is simple and makes sense.
   - b. Juan clearly has a right to the princess under the law.
   - c. Juan's argument confuses him but sounds good.

B. *Looking Back*

Discuss these questions about the story.

1. Why does Juan decide to leave his city and go into the world to seek his fortune?

2. Why is finding the centavo lucky for Juan?

3. Why do the people in the story let Juan take their things?

C. Understanding Juan's Arguments

What arguments does Juan use to get the things he wants? Complete the chart. The first one is done for you.

What Juan Wants	Juan's Argument
The chicken:	*The chicken eats his cake. The cake is now inside the chicken. So to get back the cake, he has to take the chicken.*
The dog:	
The iron bar:	
The river:	
The princess:	

Exploring the Meaning

A. Getting the Deeper Meaning

Discuss these questions about the story.

1. What is your opinion about the arguments Juan gives for claiming everything, even the princess, as his own?

2. Do you think that Juan believes in the reasons that he gives, or do you think he is just thinking of ways to get what he wants?

3. Give reasons why Juan's way of building a fortune is honest or dishonest.

4. How is this story different from what happens in most folktales? Why is the story funny?

B. Dramatizing the Story

Act out the scene that takes place at the end of the story. With two other students, take the roles of Juan, the princess, and the king.
Include these events in your scene:

- the princess tells how she met Juan and why she brings him to the king
- Juan tells why the princess belongs to him
- the king makes his decision

You may want to write out the dialogue before presenting the scene in front of the class.

C. In Everyday Life

Discuss these questions.

1. We sometimes hear about poor people marrying into very rich families. What problems might such marriages face? Give reasons for your point of view.

2. Juan has a bad habit of gambling. People find it very difficult to stop a bad habit once it starts. What can you do to stop bad habits or to help someone stop a bad habit?

The Blue Rose

Chinese

*China is a huge country in eastern Asia. About one fifth of all
the people in the world live in China. It has the world's oldest
living civilization, dating back as far as 5000 B.C. The Chinese
people are proud of their long history and the influence that
they have had on other countries. Some of the world's oldest
and finest examples of painting, pottery, porcelain, and litera-
ture are from China. In "The Blue Rose," beautiful pieces
of Chinese artwork are offered to the emperor's daughter.
Compare this love story with "How Juan Married a Princess,"
the Filipino folktale, and "The Love Crystal," the Vietnamese
folktale.*

Before You Read

Discuss these questions.

1. What colors are roses? Are there any blue roses?
2. Why do people around the world give flowers as gifts? Why do artists
   so often put flowers in their artwork?
3. Why would anybody ask for a blue rose?

Understanding Key Words

Read the sentences. You will find the words in **bold** in the story. Discuss what each word means.

1. The emperor wants his daughter to marry a **suitable** man. He wants her to marry a man he likes and thinks well of.

2. Many men try to **win the hand of** the princess. They want to marry her.

3. The shopkeeper says he is sorry, but he has no blue rose for the merchant. He **apologizes** to the merchant.

4. The King of the Five Rivers has **rare treasures** in his palace. He has very valuable works of arts that cannot be found anywhere else.

5. The warrior says to the king, "I will kill you if you do not give me the blue rose." The warrior **threatens** to kill the king.

6. The shopkeeper puts a white rose into red **dye**. The dye changes the white rose into a bright blue one.

7. The princess says everyone is **color-blind.** They cannot see that the color of the rose is blue.

Words about the Time and Place

You will find these words in the story.

astrologer	a person who studies the stars. Astrologers say that they can tell a person's future by studying the stars.
lord chamberlain	the person who manages a palace
merchant	a person whose job is to buy and sell things
pharmacy	a store where people can buy medicines and drugs
porcelain	a type of very fine dish. Porcelain dishes are usually a milky white and have paintings on them.
sapphire	a valuable, shiny stone that is usually blue in color. Like a diamond, a sapphire is a precious stone.
silk	a soft, shiny, smooth cloth. It is made from the threads spun by silkworms.
wizard	a person with magical powers, a kind of magician

The Blue Rose

Once upon a time a wise emperor in China had one daughter. She was famous as a perfect beauty who had the smallest feet in the world and lovely brown eyes. Her laughter was like a tinkling stream or the chimes of a silver bell. She was not only beautiful, but also wise. But her father, the emperor, was old, and before he died, he hoped to see her married to a suitable man.

As soon as it became known that the emperor was seeking a son-in-law, many men came to the palace to try to win his daughter's hand in marriage. The lord chamberlain told them that the emperor had decided that the man who found and brought back the blue rose would marry his daughter. But what was the blue rose and where could it be found?

Some of the men who wanted to win the princess's hand began to try to find the blue rose. One was a very rich merchant who went to the largest shop in the city and said, "I want the best blue rose you have." The shopkeeper apologized and explained he had many white, pink, and yellow roses, but no blue roses.

"Well," said the rich merchant, "you must get one for me. I do not mind how much it costs, but I must have a blue rose." The shopkeeper said he would do his best, but feared that it would be very expensive and very difficult to find.

Meanwhile, another man, a brave warrior, marched into the territory of the king of the Five Rivers. The warrior had heard this was the richest king in the world, who had the rarest treasures. He ordered the king of the Five Rivers to give him the blue rose and threatened him with a terrible fate if he did not produce it.

The King of the Five Rivers, who hated soldiers and violence, called his servant and ordered him to bring the blue rose. The servant soon returned carrying a silk cushion. On it was a large sapphire that was carved to imitate a rose with petals.

"This," said the King of the Five Rivers, "is a blue rose. You may have it."

The warrior thanked the king and went straight to the emperor's palace. When the emperor heard his story and saw the blue rose he had brought, he called his daughter to his side and said, "This brave warrior says that he has brought you the blue rose."

The princess took the precious stone in her hands and examined it. Then she said, "This is not a rose at all. It is a sapphire. I do not need any precious stones." She returned the stone to the warrior and thanked him. The warrior left sadly disappointed.

When the merchant heard about the warrior's failure, he wanted even more to win the princess's hand. He went to the shopkeeper and said, "Have you found the blue rose? I hope that you have. If you have not, I shall have you killed."

The shopkeeper said, "Sir, give three days and I promise to get the rose for you." When the merchant left, the shopkeeper became very worried, because he knew there was no blue rose. He told his wife that his life would be over if he did not find the blue rose. She told him, "If there is no blue rose, we must make one. Go to the pharmacy. Buy a strong dye that will change a white rose into a blue one."

So the shopkeeper did as she suggested and asked the pharmacist for dye. The pharmacist gave the shopkeeper a bottle of red liquid. He told the shopkeeper to dip the stem of a white rose into the liquid. Then the white rose would turn blue. The shopkeeper followed the pharmacist's directions, and the rose turned a beautiful blue. He took it to the merchant, who went immediately to the palace. The merchant confidently announced that he had found the blue rose.

The merchant was brought to the emperor. As soon as the emperor saw the blue rose, he sent for his daughter and told her, "This rich merchant claims he has brought you the blue rose. Has he found the rose you wish?"

The princess took the flower in her hands and examined it. Then she said, "This is a white rose. Its stem has been dipped into a poisonous dye that turned it blue. If a butterfly settled on it, it would die from the smell of the dye." She thanked the merchant for his effort. And the merchant left, angry and disappointed.

Many other men tried to find the blue rose. Some traveled all over the world searching for it. Others went to astrologers and wizards. But all of them failed to find the blue rose.

At last, everyone gave up, except the lord chief justice. He told the most famous artist in the country, "Make me a china cup that is white and perfectly shaped. Paint a blue rose on it."

The artist worked for two months on the lord chief justice's cup. There had never been such a beautiful cup, so perfectly shaped, so delicate. On it, the artist painted a blue rose that seemed to be picked in fairyland. It floated on the milky surface of the porcelain. When the lord justice saw it, he was very pleased.

He went to the palace, and he told the emperor that he had brought the blue rose. When the emperor saw it, he sent for his daughter. "The lord chief justice says that he has brought you the blue rose," said the emperor. "Has he found the rose you are searching for?" he asked.

The princess examined the cup and said, "This is the most beautiful piece of china that I have ever seen. Please allow me to keep it until I find the blue rose. It is so beautiful that no other flower should be put in it except the blue rose."

The lord chief justice thanked the princess for accepting his cup but left disappointed.

After this, there was no one who dared to find the blue rose.

One day a traveling musician visited the country. One summer evening he was playing his lute near a wall and singing whatever came to his head. The sun was just going down, and one or two stars were twinkling in the sky. The musician sang about his joy in the beauty of the sunset.

As the musician looked up, he saw a pale, thin figure calling him. He walked along the wall until he came to a gate. There was someone waiting for him who gently led him into the shadow of a dark tree. In the twilight, he saw two eyes and understood the message. A thousand words were whispered in the light of the stars, and the hours passed quickly. It was the princess. When the east began to grow light, she said it was time to go.

"Tomorrow, I shall come to the palace to ask for your hand," said the musician.

"I wish that was possible," said the princess, "but my father has said the man I marry must find the blue rose."

"That is simple," said the musician. "I will find it." And they said good night to each other.

The next morning the musician picked a white rose on his way to the palace. He was brought to the emperor, who called his daughter. The emperor told his daughter, "This poor musician says that he has brought you the blue rose. Has he found the rose you are searching for?"

The princess took the rose in her hands and said, "Yes, he has found the blue rose."

When everyone pointed out that this was an ordinary white rose and not a blue one, the princess answered, "I think the rose is blue. Perhaps all of you are color-blind."

The emperor decided that if the princess thought the rose was blue, it was blue. Everyone knew that she could see beauty better than anyone else in the land.

So the musician married the princess, and they lived in a little house on the sea coast with a garden full of white roses and they lived happily ever after. The emperor knew that his daughter had married whom she loved, and so he died in peace.

Understanding the Story

A. *When Does It Happen?*

Show the order in which the events in the story happen. Write the correct number in the blank.

_____ The lord chief justice brings a porcelain cup with a beautiful blue rose painted on it.

_____ The princess marries the musician.

_____ The princess says she does not need any precious stones.

_____ A warrior brings a beautiful blue sapphire carved to look like a blue rose.

__1__ The lord chamberlain announces that the princess will marry the man who brings a blue rose.

_____ The princess invites the musician to come into the garden.

_____ The merchant brings the princess a white rose that has been dyed blue.

_____ The musician brings a white rose that the princess says is blue.

B. *Looking Back*

Discuss these questions about the story.

1. Why does the emperor want his daughter to get married?

2. No one can find a real blue rose. What does the merchant bring instead? What does the warrior bring? What does the lord chief justice bring?

3. Why doesn't the princess accept any of these "blue roses"?

4. Why does she say the musician brought her the blue rose she wants?

5. What excuse does she give for saying that a white rose is blue?

C. *Understanding the Stories of Two Characters*

The mandarin's daughter in "The Love Crystal" and the Chinese princess fall in love with musicians. Contrast the two folktales. Complete the chart.

Situation	The Mandarin's Daughter in "The Love Crystal"	The Chinese Princess in "The Blue Rose"
How does the young woman's father feel about her meeting men?	*He does not want her to meet men so he shuts her up in a tower.*	
How does the princess act when she hears the young man's song?		
What happens when the princess meets the musician?		
What kind of ending does the story have?		
How could the story have ended differently?		

Exploring the Meaning

A. *Getting the Deeper Meaning*

Discuss these questions about the story.

1. If there are no blue roses, why does the emperor say that the man who marries his daughter must first bring her a blue rose?

2. Why does the princess say no to each offer of a blue rose?

3. Why is the princess interested in the musician, but not in the other men who bring her blue roses?

4. Why does the emperor allow his daughter to marry the musician?

5. How do we know that the emperor loves his daughter?

6. What lesson does the story teach?

B. *Adding New Endings*

Discuss the following.

1. What might have happened if the Chinese princess did not invite the musician into her garden?

2. What might have happened if the emperor did not agree that the musician's rose was blue?

3. Describe the life of the musician and the princess after they have been married for several years.

C. *In Everyday Life*

Discuss these questions.

1. Should parents allow their children to marry partners of their own choice, or should they try to influence their children's decisions? Give reasons for your point of view.

2. Should young people meet boyfriends and girlfriends secretly, or should they tell parents about whom they are dating? Give reasons for your point of view.

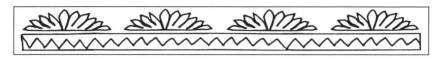

PART FOUR

Death and Inheritance

A True Hero

Mexican

Mexico is a country in Latin America. Spanish is its official language, although many people sometimes use their traditional Indian languages. Most people of Mexico are descended from the Indian tribes that have lived there for many centuries and from the Spaniards who arrived early in the sixteenth century. In this story from Mexico, a father has to decide to which of his three sons to give a valuable possession. Before you read the ending, try to guess which son he will give it to.

Before You Read

Discuss these questions.

1. What do you know about the life of the Aztecs or other Indian tribes that lived in Mexico?
2. Why do you think this story is called "The True Hero"?
3. In real life, who do you think is a true hero?

Understanding Key Words

Read the sentences. You will find the words in **bold** in the story. Discuss what each word means.

1. The diamond is the only **wealth** that the man has. He has nothing else that can be sold for a lot of money.

2. The diamond has been in the family for **generations.** It belonged to his father and before that to his grandfather and before that to his great-grandfather.

3. The father wants to see who would do the most good. He wants to see which of his sons would **accomplish** the best deed.

4. The son wants to do something **worthy** of receiving the diamond. He wants to do something that is good enough to earn the diamond.

5. One son almost **drowns** trying to save a girl from the river. He nearly dies in the water trying to save the girl.

6. He **risks his life** trying to save the young girl. He could have died trying to get her out of the water.

7. The two men **weep** when they understand what happened. They cry because of the strong emotions they feel.

8. The two men **swear** they will be friends forever. They promise very sincerely that they will always be friends.

Words about the Time and Place

You will find these words in the story.

cliff	a side of a mountain that goes straight up and down, like a wall
Guadalajara	a city in western Mexico. It is Mexico's second largest city.
Rio Grande River	the river that is the border between the United States and Mexico

---

A True Hero

Once there was a very old man in Guadalajara who was about to die. He wanted to leave a diamond, the only wealth he had, to one of his three sons. But he could not decide which one should get it. He called the three sons into his room and told them:

"My sons, I am not a rich man. The only thing I have that is worth much is this diamond. It has been in our family for generations, and I would not want it to be sold. Because it cannot be sold or divided, I can give it to only one of you. I will give the diamond to the one who accomplishes the greatest good in a week's time. Go now. Return in a week to tell me what you have done."

A week passed and the sons returned. They found their father even weaker than before and unable to leave his bed. He asked each son to tell what he had done.

"My father," said the first son, "I thought and thought of what I could do that would be worthy. Finally this is what I did. I made list of all my property, divided it in half, and gave one half to the poor people in this city."

The old man shook his head, "Ah, that is good, but not good enough. Everyone should help the poor as much as possible."

"Father," said the second son, "when I was returning home from work one day, I saw a little girl caught in the Rio Grande River. I can hardly swim, but I jumped into the river. I almost drowned, but I pulled the girl out and saved her life."

"That is good too. Everyone should be willing to risk one's life to save a child."

Then the third son told what happened to him. "Father, a wonderful thing happened to me. One morning I saw a man wrapped in a blanket, sleeping at the edge of a cliff. If he moved at all in his sleep, he would certainly fall over the cliff, thousands of feet down into the valley below! I came quietly closer, because I didn't want to frighten him. And guess who the man was? Sancho, my worst en-

emy! He had threatened many times to kill me if he had a chance.

"I moved as close as I could to the man. I put my arms gently around him. Suddenly his eyes opened and he looked into mine. I saw that he was afraid, so I told him not to be afraid and I rolled him away from the cliff.

"He told me that he had come that way the night before. It was so dark and he was too tired to continue. So he walked off the path and went to sleep. He had no idea where he was. If he had walked any farther or turned in his sleep, he would have been killed. Sancho said, 'You saved my life—friend—after I threatened to kill you!'

"We went into one another's arms and swore to be friends forever. We wept and understood that each of us found a friend, although we had been enemies before."

The old man said, "This is a beautiful story and an example of someone becoming a hero by a good action. Very few men will risk their lives to help the enemy. You are a truly great man. This diamond is yours."

Understanding the Story

A. What Happens?

Match the sentence parts. Write the correct letter in each blank.

____ 1. The old man is	a.	the diamond to one son.
____ 2. Each son hopes	b.	going to die.
____ 3. The first son gives	c.	his enemy from falling off the cliff.
____ 4. The second son saves	d.	half of his things to the poor.
____ 5. The third son saves	e.	a girl from drowning.
____ 6. The father gives	f.	to get the diamond.

B. Looking Back

Discuss these questions about the story.

1. What problem does the father have?
2. Why does the father give the sons only one week to accomplish a great deed?
3. Why does the father say that the first son did not earn the diamond?
4. Why does the father say that the second son did not earn the diamond?
5. Why does the father think the third son earned the diamond?

C. *Remembering the Characters' Actions*

Complete the chart.

Person	What He Did
The dying old father:	*He says he will give the diamond to the son who does the greatest deed.*
The first son:	
The second son:	
The third son:	
At the end, the old father:	

Exploring the Meaning

A. *Getting the Deeper Meaning*

Discuss these questions about the story.

1. Why does the father want to give his inheritance to the son who will do the greatest good? Do you think this is a good way to decide?

2. Children usually inherit their parents' wealth only after the parents die. Why does the old man want to give the diamond away before he dies?

3. Do you think the other two sons will accept their father's decision or be jealous of their brother who got the diamond?

B. *Debating the Issues*

1. Do you agree or disagree with the father's decision to give the diamond to the third son? Discuss this in small groups or as a class. Take these positions:

   - why the first son should get the diamond
   - why the second son should get the diamond
   - why the third son should get the diamond
   - why some other solution is best (for example, selling the diamond and dividing the money in three ways)

2. Who is a true hero? First, as a class, brainstorm a list of four or five heroes. Next, each student should decide which hero he or she thinks is the greatest. Then, form into groups of students who have chosen the same "greatest hero." Have a debate in which each group explains why the person it has chosen is a true hero.

3. Compare the third son's heroism with the heroism of the daughter in "The Woodsman's Daughter and the Lion" (see pages 49–52). Which one do you think was braver? Give reasons for your decision. Compare your answer with other answers in your group or with a partner's opinion.

C. *In Everyday Life*

Discuss these questions.

1. A will is a legal paper stating what a person wants done with his or her property after he or she dies. What problems can happen in a family when a will is read?

2. What advice do you have for parents about wills? Can they prepare their wills so that there will be less jealousy and anger in a family?

A Chief Names His Heirs

West African

The Ashanti people are the largest and most powerful group in the West African country of Ghana. A large number of popular folktales come from the Ashanti. Many of these folktales tell about a spider named Anansi. Anansi often tries to trick others but usually gets into trouble himself. But the folktale you are going to read is a more serious one. It is about the chief of a tribe and what will happen to his property when he dies.

Before You Read

Discuss these questions.

1. What do you know about life in West Africa?
2. Who do you think will be the heirs (inheritors) of the chief of a tribe?

Understanding Key Words

Read the sentences. You will find the words in **bold** in the story. Discuss what each word means.

1. Everyone wants to know to whom the chief is going to give his property. They want to know who his **heir** is going to be.

2. The chief wants his wealth to be **distributed** to good people. He wants it to be divided and given to people who will use it correctly.

3. In the **tradition** of the people, the nephew is the heir to the chief. For many years, it is the tribe's practice that the nephew will receive the chief's property when he dies.

4. The chief's **possessions** include land, storehouses, servants, and slaves. All these belong to him.

5. The chief does not want his workers to be **abused.** The chief does not want the workers to be treated badly by their new owner.

6. The nephew feels that his uncle is **rejecting** him. He thinks the chief is not satisfied with him and does not trust him.

7. The people in the village feel that it is a great **injustice** not to give the nephew his uncle's wealth. They feel it is not right that the nephew does not receive his correct part.

8. The people of the village are **witnesses** to what the nephew chooses. They all hear the nephew's decision.

9. The nephew does not want to be **accused** of wasting his uncle's wealth. He doesn't want people to say that he will use his uncle's possessions in a bad way.

Words about the Time and Place

You will find these words in the story.

servant a person who works in someone's house and is paid for the work

slave a person who is someone's property and can be bought and sold. A slave works without pay.

spokesman a person who speaks for someone else

A Chief Names His Heirs

T here was a chief living in Dagomba. He was growing old, so he began to think of how his possessions would be distributed when he died. According to the traditions of those times, a man's possessions were not given to his son. Instead they were given to his sister's son: his nephew. The chief had much wealth: large fields, storehouses filled with corn, and many servants and slaves. He wondered if his nephew would be able to take care of all these possessions wisely. He said to himself, "How do I know that my nephew will not let the fields go uncared for, abuse my slaves, and waste everything?"

One day when he felt that his life was growing short, the chief sent for his nephew and said to him, "My nephew, you are the one who is supposed to inherit from me. I want you to inherit thoughtfully. When I am dead and my property is given away, you will select one thing that I own and claim it for yourself. Everything else I will leave to my head slave, for he has been very loyal and faithful to me all my life. I speak of it now so that you will have time to decide what you want most."

The nephew went away thinking, "What makes my uncle behave this way? Am I not his nephew? He tells me 'Inherit thoughtfully. Take only one thing.' Shall I take his gun or his garden, or the tree in his yard and leave everything else of value to his head slave?" The nephew was worried. He thought, "Why should I even attend the meeting where his will is made public? No, he rejects me, so I want nothing from him at all."

But the young man could not get these thoughts out of his mind. He did not eat. He did not sleep. He told his mother, "My uncle is putting me aside. He says, 'Take one thing from my possessions. The rest I will give to my head slave.'" His mother answered: "Perhaps there is some meaning in it that you do not understand. He may be testing you." The young man thought about it, but he could not find an answer.

The chief died. They buried him and had a funeral feast. The time came when the chief's spokesman was going to announce how the

possessions would be distributed. People of the town gathered in front of the chief's house. The nephew also came because an answer had appeared to him that night in a dream.

The chief's spokesman announced to the crowd that the nephew could select one thing and that all the rest would go to the head slave. When the people heard that, they were angry. They said, "It is an injustice. It has never happened that a man refused to let a nephew have his rightful inheritance."

The nephew spoke, "I have thought deeply about this matter. I thought perhaps I would not come, or that I would say 'Give everything to the slave, because he has been a faithful servant to my uncle.' But my uncle said to me, 'Inherit thoughtfully.' He wanted to be sure I would not waste his fields and storehouses by not caring for them. But I shall do as he wished. I shall choose one thing: my uncle's head slave."

The chief's spokesman announced to the crowd: "You are witnesses. The nephew chooses the head slave. The head slave receives everything else." And the crowd called out: "We are witnesses!"

The spokesman said: "It has been witnessed. Although the nephew inherits one man, he inherits everything, because the property of a slave is the property of the master. What a slave owns, the master owns. Nephew, you have inherited thoughtfully, as the chief wished. This is what we say to you:

Do not waste what has been given to you.

Never say, "With my own effort I created all this property."

Do not abuse your workers, because they put food in your mouth.

When a tool breaks, we put a new blade in it.

You are the new blade. May your fields grow very well.

As you inherited thoughtfully, live thoughtfully.

And the nephew answered:

"Sir, I accept my inheritance with thankfulness. My uncle's head slave was sure he would inherit wealth, and now he finds he has nothing. Will anyone accuse me of wasting my inheritance if I give this man a field, a house, and a storehouse of his own?"

The chief spokesman said, "No, they will praise you for an honorable action."

So the chief's inheritance was settled, and his words to his nephew became a saying: "Inherit thoughtfully."

Understanding the Story

A. What Happens?

Complete each sentence by choosing **a, b,** or **c.** Circle the letter of the answer you think is correct.

1. The chief wants to plan his will because
    a. he wants to be sure his nephew gets everything.
    b. he doesn't want his nephew to get anything.
    c. he wonders if his nephew will take good care of the possessions.

2. As the chief's life is ending, he tells his nephew,
    a. "When I am dead, my property will be given to you."
    b. "When I am dead, select one thing that I own and take it."
    c. "When I am dead, my head slave will receive everything."

3. The nephew thinks at first,
    a. "My uncle rejects me, so I don't want anything of his."
    b. "My uncle rejects me, so I am very angry at him."
    c. "My uncle rejects me, so I am very disappointed."

4. After his uncle's death, the nephew asks only for the head slave because
    a. he automatically gets everything else the uncle owned.
    b. his mother warns him that this is the only way to get his uncle's possessions.
    c. he knows the slave could help him reach great wealth.

5. At the end the father's faithful slave receives
    a. nothing.
    b. a field, a house, and a storehouse from the nephew.
    c. the possessions the chief left him: large fields, storehouses filled with corn, and many slaves and servants.

B. Looking Back

Discuss these questions about the story.

1. What tradition of inheritance do the people of Dagomba follow?

2. What does the chief tell his nephew he plans to do with his property?

3. What thoughts run through the nephew's mind after he hears his uncle's plan?

4. What does the chief's spokesman tell the crowd after the chief's death?

5. What is the nephew's reply to the spokesman's announcement about the chief's will?

C. Understanding the Parts of the Story

Complete the chart. The chart shows the main parts of the story.

The characters in the story:	
Where the story takes place:	
Problems: 1. The chief's problem at the beginning of the story: 2. The nephew's problem after he learns he will receive only one thing:	1. 2.
What happens at the end of the story:	

Exploring the Meaning

A. Getting the Deeper Meaning

Discuss these questions about the story.

1. Why does the chief decide to test his nephew before giving him all his possessions?

2. Why does the nephew's mother, not the nephew himself, understand that his uncle is testing him?

3. What does the nephew's decision about the inheritance show?

4. Why are the villagers angered by the chief's decision not to give everything to the nephew?

5. What do the nephew's actions at the end of the story show?

B. Telling the Story Again

Imagine that you are one of the people of Dagomba who hears the will of the chief and the nephew's decision. You are telling the story to someone from another town.

Tell about the following:

- how people felt when they heard the will
- what you thought was going to happen
- what one thing the nephew selected
- what this means he will get
- how people felt at the end

C. In Everyday Life

Discuss these questions.

1. How is property passed from one generation to the next in your country?

2. Sometimes parents do not leave their property for their children. For what reasons might they decide to give their possessions to someone else?

3. If you inherited a lot of property or money from your parents, what would you do with it?

The Skeleton's Dance

Japanese

Many folktales tell about friendship or love between two people. Sometimes one of the friends or lovers is faithful and true, but the other is untrue and hurts the one who is loyal. This story from Japan, in eastern Asia, is about two men who are friends. It is a tale of good versus bad.

Before You Read

Discuss these questions.

1. What stories or songs do you know about people who had a friend or lover who hurt them?
2. If you have already read "How Juan Married a Princess" (see pages 112–114), what do you think might happen to the character in this story who is a gambler?
3. What do you expect when you hear the word "skeleton" in the title of a story? What kind of story will it be?

Understanding Key Words

Read the sentences. You will find the words in **bold** in the story. Discuss what each word means.

1. Shimo has bad **companions.** The friends with whom he spends his time are not good people.

2. Shimo's friends do **evil** things. They steal other people's property and spend it on drinking and gambling.

3. When the skeleton dances, it **rattles and clatters.** The bones make noise as they hit one another.

4. The skeleton promises Shimo that there will be no **expense** for him. Because he is dead, there will be no cost for his food or clothing.

5. When Shimo gets angry, he begins to **curse.** He shouts out bad words in anger.

6. The skeleton **bows** before the lord. He bends low to show respect.

7. The skeleton speaks **humbly** to the lord. He shows the lord great respect.

Words about the Time and Place

You will find these words in the story.

dice   a pair of small cubes with a number of spots on each side. They are used in various games, often for gambling.

kimono   the traditional clothing of Japan. It is a big, loose robe held in place by a wide sash (cloth belt) at the waist.

lord   a person who has power. Usually lords own much land.

province   a division of a country

throne   a special chair for a king or queen. It is usually used during ceremonies.

whip   a piece of thin leather, often used to hit animals to make them move

---

The Skeleton's Dance

Many years ago in Japan, there were two young men, Kami and Shimo, who were good friends. They decided to go to another country to find work.

Shimo worked very hard and earned a great deal of money, but Kami quickly fell in with a bunch of bad companions and did nothing except waste his days with evil pleasures. At night, he got drunk and noisy, and he learned the ways of thieves and murderers.

After three years, Shimo decided to return home and asked his friend to join him. Kami answered, "I really do want to go back, but I have no clothes for the trip."

Since they had left their home village together, Shimo did not want to leave Kami and go home alone. So he gave Kami enough money for clothes and some traveling money. Together they set out. However, when they got to the mountain pass just before their village, Kami attacked Shimo, killed him, and took his money. Pretending that nothing had happened, Kami returned to his home in the village.

The villagers greeted Kami warmly. Many asked, "How is your good friend, Shimo?" Kami told all the villagers this story: "Shimo changed into a completely different person after he left the village. From the day he arrived until this day, he has done nothing but waste his money in the company of the most wicked men. So he had no money for traveling expenses and could not return home."

Soon after this, Kami began to gamble and play dice. In a short time, he had lost all the money he had taken from Shimo, so he set off for another country. On his way, he traveled to the same mountain pass where he had killed his friend Shimo. As he was going through the pass, he heard a voice calling, "Kami, Kami." Wondering who it was, he looked around, but could see no one. Thinking that he only imagined that he had heard something, he continued on his way. But he had only gone a few steps when the voice called out again, "Kami, Kami!"

"Well, this is surely strange," Kami thought. Looking into the bushes, Kami discovered a skeleton on the ground. While Kami looked on in surprise, the skeleton laughed loudly with its white teeth, got up, and turned toward him. It said, "Has it been such a long time that you have forgotten me, my friend? I am Shimo, whom you robbed and killed here three years ago. I have been waiting here, hoping that I would meet you again someday. Today my wish has come true."

Kami was very much surprised and tried to run away, but the skeleton seized his kimono in its bony hand, and it would not let go.

"Where are you going now?" asked the skeleton. "Tell me what you have been doing since you killed me."

Kami had no choice but to tell the truth. "I went home to the village, but the money soon disappeared, so I set out on a trip to look for work, and here I am. Please let me go."

"I see that you haven't changed. You are always in trouble," said the skeleton. "I have an idea. I can dance like this." And the skeleton began to dance, rattling and clattering its bones together, waving its arms in the air and kicking with its legs. "Why don't you take me along with you? You can put me in a box and carry me around with you, and people will pay you to see me dance. Since I won't eat or wear clothes, and money means nothing to me, you can earn a great deal without any expense."

The skeleton continued, "Well, Kami, that's how it will be. If you sing and call the tune, I can dance any kind of dance you want. What do you say? We could make a lot of money, couldn't we?"

Kami agreed that it would be a good way to make a lot of money, and so he took the skeleton and continued on his way.

Reports of Kami and his dancing skeleton spread from town to village, and even the lord of the country heard about them. Kami was called to come to the lord's castle. The lord told him to have the skeleton dance in the huge hall that was filled with his guests.

Kami opened the box, but the skeleton would not do a single dance for the lord. Kami played tune after tune, he turned blue, then red; and he sang various songs. Then he began to yell and curse, but the skeleton refused to move.

Finally Kami became so angry that he took his whip and began to beat the skeleton. Then it got up and stood before the lord. Bowing humbly, it said, "My lord, I have been dancing all the time, just so that I would be brought before you. This fellow killed me and robbed me of my money, although I was an honest citizen of your province." Then the skeleton told exactly what had happened.

The lord, who was a just man, was surprised by the way Kami had treated his loyal friend. "Quick, tie that man with a rope, and take him away to be tried!" he ordered his guards. And just at that moment, the skeleton fell to pieces before the throne.

Three days later Kami was sentenced to death for his crimes.

Understanding the Story

A. *When Does It Happen?*

Show the order in which the events in the story happen. Write the correct number in the blank.

__1__ Shimo gives Kami money to return to their village with him.

____ The skeleton refuses to dance for the lord.

____ Kami kills Shimo.

____ The skeleton tells the lord that Kami killed him.

____ Kami meets a skeleton that says it is Shimo.

____ The skeleton goes with Kami everywhere to dance and make money for him.

B. *Looking Back*

Discuss these questions about the story.

1. Why does Kami have no money to return to his village with Shimo?
2. Why does Shimo help out his friend?
3. What lie does Kami tell the villagers about his friend Shimo?
4. How does the skeleton convince Kami to take it with him?
5. How does Shimo get Kami destroyed?

C. *Contrasting Two Characters*

Describe Shimo and Kami. You can use the list at the bottom of the chart. Add some ideas of your own.

Shimo	Kami
works hard	

doesn't want to work   lies a lot   likes to gamble
is generous   is loyal to a friend   works hard

Exploring the Meaning

A. *Getting the Deeper Meaning*

Discuss these questions about the story.

1. How does Shimo's murder make you feel about Shimo and Kami?

2. Why does Shimo's skeleton offer to help Kami make money by dancing?

3. Why does the skeleton plan to be invited to dance for the lord of the province?

4. Why is Kami's being sentenced to death a good ending for this folktale?

5. What does the story tell about good and evil?

B. *Newspaper Article*

Imagine that you are a reporter for a newspaper. You are at the lord's feast when the skeleton tells its story. Write a newspaper article about the feast. Tell about these events:

- what you saw and heard at the feast
- the story told by the skeleton
- what happened to Kami

C. *In Everyday Life*

Discuss these questions.

1. How can a person stop a bad habit such as gambling, smoking, or taking drugs?

2. Why do some people believe in ghosts, haunted houses, or speaking with the dead?

3. How does a person know if a friend can be trusted?

The Voyage Below the Water

Haitian

Haiti is a French-speaking country in the Caribbean Sea. Haitians are descendants of Africans, who were first brought to the island as slaves. Many Haitians follow a religion called "Vodoun" that the slaves took with them from West Africa. They believe the world is full of unseen gods and spirits of their dead ancestors. They try to protect themselves from the spirits by wearing magical charms and performing certain ceremonies.

This story is about a man whose wife has just died. How can he deal with the grief that the loss of his wife brings to him?

Before You Read

Discuss these questions.

1. What customs and traditions does your homeland have about connections between the living and the dead? Are the dead remembered in ceremonies, prayers, or on a special holiday?
2. What "voyage below the water" do you think this story will tell about?

Understanding Key Words

Read the sentences. You will find the words in **bold** in the story. Discuss what each word means.

1. When Bordeau's wife dies, she is buried in a **coffin.** It is a box made of brown wood.

2. **Prayers** are said for the dead woman. The people ask the gods to take good care of her.

3. Bordeau's **grief** for his wife does not end. He feels great sadness all the time.

4. No family **escapes** death. Someone in every family will die at some time.

5. When Bordeau's wife dies, she joins all her **ancestors** in the world under the sea. She goes to live with all the family members who have died before her.

6. Bordeau cannot be **persuaded** to stop grieving. No one can convince him to stop crying for her. He does not change his mind.

Words about the Time and Place

You will find these words in the story.

drummer	a person who plays the drum. The drum is a round musical instrument used to make a rhythmic sound.
feast	a large, special meal
kerchief	a piece of cloth for wiping the face or for covering one's head
mahogany	a strong reddish wood. It is often used to make fine furniture.
rattle	an object that is shaken to make noise. It is used in the religious ceremonies of the Haitians.
sacred	holy or special to the gods
sacrifice	something special given to the gods

The Voyage Below the Water

There was a man named Bordeau who lived in the country. He had worked hard all his life, and he became wealthy. He had many children. He was happy. Then, one day, his wife died.

There were the ceremonies. He had a mahogany coffin made. She was buried.

Bordeau hardly said a word. He sat in his house silently. If the children spoke, he did not seem to hear. The sons went out to take care of the fields, but Bordeau did not go with them. His old friends came to pass an hour or two with him in the evening, but he said nothing. When food was brought to him, he refused to eat. He didn't seem to know whether it was day or night.

The time went by. The evening arrived for the saying of last prayer for the dead woman. Relatives and friends came from the villages. The "houngan," the Vodoun religious leader, came. And the drummers came. And as they were preparing for the praying, dancing, and singing in the courtyard, Bordeau came out of the house and asked them all to go home.

"Bordeau," one of his old friends said, "this is the night of the last prayers. Do not send the people home. Let us hold the service." Bordeau answered, "For the praying, the singing, the dancing, and the feast, I care nothing. What does all this mean to me now that my wife is gone? Go away. I cannot bear the sound of music. I will not dance, I will not eat. My grief is too great."

"Bordeau," one of his friends said, "death comes to every family. No one escapes. Today it is there. Tomorrow it is here."

Another one said, "Bordeau, the dead cannot return. Do not treat yourself this way. Let the last prayers be said. Let the people dance. And let the feast be held."

"No," Bordeau said. "My house shall remain silent."

"Bordeau," the houngan said, "your wife now lives beneath the water with the ancestors. We do not give ourselves to silence and grief forever because the one we love has gone there.''

But Bordeau was not persuaded.

So the houngan said: "Bordeau, I will go under the water to find your wife. I will try to speak with her.''

"Very well," Bordeau said. "But if you do not bring her back, then I will not speak again, I will not eat, my land can grow back to wild grass, and my house can rot and fall where it stands."

The houngan made preparations. He took his sacred rattle in his hand and went down to the edge of the river. The people brought animals to sacrifice. There was a ceremony. They sang. And at midnight the houngan walked slowly into the river, deeper and deeper, until he disappeared.

The people waited on the bank of the river for three days, and at midnight of the third day, the houngan came out of the river, shaking his sacred rattle. There was great excitement. The people took him to Bordeau's house. They entered. Bordeau was sitting there.

"He has returned!" the people shouted to Bordeau. "Our houngan has gone below the water and come back!"

"Where is my wife?" Bordeau asked.

"Listen, Bordeau," the houngan said. "I went below the water. I went far. There was a long road. I followed it. There were hills, and I crossed them. There was a forest, and I passed through it. I came to the City of the Ancestors. There were many, many people there. My father was among them. My mother was among them. Your father and mother were there. Your grandfathers were there. Everyone who was ever here before us was there. I searched for your wife. I went everywhere. I came to the marketplace, and there

I found her selling beans. I said, "Your husband Bordeau is grieving. He does not eat, he does not sleep, he does not speak. He says, 'If my wife does not return from the dead, may my house fall in upon me.' I have come to bring you back. Your wife said this Bordeau. She said, 'It is pleasant to have someone grieve for you. But I live here now, below the water. When one dies, he does not return. Tell Bordeau to bring the grief to an end. Tell him to eat. For when one is dead, one is dead, but when one is alive, one must live.' Bordeau, your wife gave me one of the gold earrings she wore. She said it was for you."

The houngan took his kerchief from his pocket, and from the kerchief he took an earring, which he gave to Bordeau.

Bordeau looked at the earring, saying, "Yes, this is my wife's earring."

He sat silently for a long while, looking at the earring. At last he said this:

"My wife has sent me a message from below the water. She said, 'When one is alive, one must live.' So it shall be. Let us hold the service of the last prayers. Let the food be prepared. Let the drummers drum. I will eat. I will dance."

Understanding the Story

A. What Happens?

Match the sentence parts. Write the correct letter in each blank.

____ 1. After Bordeau's wife dies,

____ 2. When Bordeau's old friends ask

____ 3. Bordeau refuses

____ 4. The houngan walks

____ 5. The houngan gives

a. to have the feast on the night of the last prayers for his wife.

b. Bordeau to stop grieving, he will not listen.

c. he becomes depressed..

d. Bordeau his wife's earring.

e. into the water and disappears.

B. *Looking Back*

Discuss these questions about the story.

1. How does Bordeau act after his wife's death?
2. How do his friends try to make him feel better?
3. What preparations are made before the houngan goes on his voyage?
4. What does the houngan tell Bordeau he has found below the water?
5. What request does the houngan bring Bordeau from his dead wife?

C. *Understanding the Characters*

Everyone in the story tries to help Bordeau because his wife is dead. Complete the chart.

When?	Who Speaks to Bordeau?	Bordeau's Answer
After the funeral:		*He doesn't even hear.*
The time of the last prayer for his wife:	His friends	
The time of the last prayer for his wife:	The houngan	
	His wife	

Exploring the Meaning

A. Getting the Deeper Meaning

Discuss these questions about the story.

1. How is Bordeau's grief different from the grief a person usually has when there is a death in the family?

2. Why does the houngan bring an earring to Bordeau?

3. The story tells us a great deal about what the Haitians believe. What beliefs about the dead do the people of Haiti have? What ceremonies are there for the dead?

4. What lesson does this story teach?

B. Your Ideas about the Character

Bordeau is the main character in this story. Work with a partner to choose the one word or phrase that you think best describes him.

- loyal
- selfish, thinking only about himself
- stubborn
- happy
- not very friendly

List three reasons why you think your choice is the best to describe Bordeau. Give examples from the story. Share your ideas with the class.

C. In Everyday Life

Discuss these questions.

1. Bordeau is depressed because he is grieving for his wife. How can depressed people be helped today?

2. What serious problems can result when a person does not come out of a period of depression?

3. How does a mourning period help a person overcome his or her deep sadness after losing a loved one?